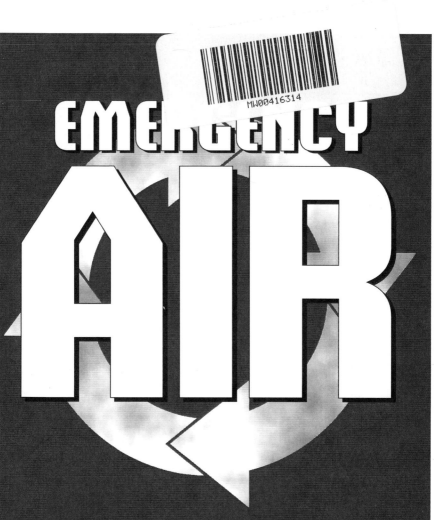

EMERGENCY AIR

For Shelter-in-Place Preppers and Home-Built Bunkers

F.J. Bohan

Paladin Press • Boulder, Colorado

Other books by F.J. Bohan
Living on the Edge
Barbed Wire, Barricades, and Bunkers

Emergency Air:
For Shelter-in-Place
Preppers and Home-Built Bunkers
by F.J. Bohan

Copyright © 2013 by F.J. Bohan

ISBN 13: 978-1-61004-867-5
Printed in the United States of America

Published by Paladin Press, a division of
Paladin Enterprises, Inc.
Gunbarrel Tech Center
7077 Winchester Circle
Boulder, Colorado 80301 USA, +1.303.443.7250

Direct inquiries and/or orders to the above address.

Visit our website at www.paladin-press.com

CONTENTS

INTRODUCTION

There are many things we can do without for extended periods, but breathable air is not one of them. All our survival plans are for naught if we're forced to do without a sufficient supply of breathable air for more than three or four minutes. Without it, you will most likely be dead in that short time. For up to half of this three-to-four minute period, you can assume that you'll be either unconscious or unable to function at a useful level.

For the survivalist or prepper considering an underground shelter or bunker, air ventilation is the most important consideration for survival. I had planned to address this issue in my earlier book *Barbed Wire, Barricades, and Bunkers*, but lacking solid information on ventilation systems at that time, I chose to do more research. Now, after much study and consideration, I am able to offer a companion book that includes not just theory, but also some home-built and tested air pump designs that anyone can build from easily obtained supplies.

Part of the challenge in preparing this book is simply that very little has been written on the subject of home-built air pumps. Of the few designs available, I found them to be somewhat complicated to build, in addition to being inefficient. Additionally, several designs looked to be so large that there would be little room left in the shelter for necessary supplies. With time, space, and money being short for everyone these days, I wanted to address how the average prepper could take affordable steps to ensure that he would be able to breathe in his underground shelter.

During the Cold War, the U.S. Department of Defense (DOD) published numerous booklets on constructing underground shelters. All of them implied that you could simply run down to the nearest hardware store and pick up a hand-crank air pump for your shelter. Sadly, this was never the case. If it had been, there would be hundreds of Cold War–era hand-crank air pumps for sale all over the country at swap meets, flea markets, and yard sales. Yet, I have been to hundreds of these events and have never seen one anywhere. Still, it is my opinion that the ideal air pump would actually be the one that DOD said was down at the hardware store, so that's where I headed to start my hands-on research for designing buried-shelter air pumps.

As it turns out, DOD was correct! There are indeed buried-shelter air pumps available at hardware stores. You just have to know what to look for and how to put them together. It is important to note that while the testing of these designs is based on solid scientific principles, the testing was conducted in my private shelter, and not by a nationally recognized testing laboratory. Further, the specifications are based on the published specifications for the relative components. Thus, the findings should be considered nonscientific. My primary testing concern was how much air the pumps moved. I sought out the best materials I could find at such stores as Lowe's, Home Depot, and Tractor Supply. If used gently, the pumps should have a reasonably long service life.

It should be also noted that the items purchased and used to make the air pumps in this book are not necessarily being used in the manner for which they were originally designed. The reader should in no way consider their use described here as being an endorsement or recommendation by the manufacturer and should understand that there are no warranties or guarantees about their performance in actual emergencies.

It is my hope that these relatively inexpensive air pump designs, along with the important information contained in this book, will help others to be prepared and safe inside their shelter-in-place locations and underground bunkers during an emergency and offer a breath of fresh air to a subject about which very little has been written.

1

A HISTORY
OF AIR PUMPS

The history of air pumps is one of the most obscure subjects ever written about—or make that *never* written about. As chronicled in historical records, the first air pumps were simply fans. Kings and noblemen in the past often relied on servants swaying either a large ostrich feather or some type of woven reed fan to move the air. This method of moving air is not credited to anyone specifically, since most people with even half a brain could have come up with the notion, but, nonetheless, history records the first improvement in air-moving techniques in 500 B.C. This is when a system of ceiling-suspended canvas fans called *punkahs* was first used in India. The lucky schmucks who got to stand along a sidewall and pull on the ropes that operated these ceiling fans were called *punkawallahs*. Variants of these types of ceiling fans are still used today—though they are not usually manually operated.

Shortly after this development, someone came up with the concept of what we know today as the bellows. Here, too, little was recorded. In fact, we're not even sure what the device was originally called. It is clear, however, that the first bellows was developed in China to aid in the manufacture of metal tools. It was during the Han Dynasty (206 B.C. to A.D. 220) that a bright, young engineer named Du Shi utilized the power of a hydraulic pump to power a bellows and effectively created the first mechanical air pump. His design was later incorporated into the first blast furnace.

Like all good ideas, the bellows was copied, and its use spread all over the world. In its heyday, the bellows was referred to by other names, including "blast bag" and "blowing bag." The word *bellows* comes from the old English word for bag, *belg*—in its plural form, *belgo*.

Few developments in the field of air pumps or bellows occurred for nearly a thousand years, until the mid-1600s. Around then Robert Boyle began to ponder the properties of air and its effect on living things. This led Boyle to do some of the first studies in air dynamics, air pumps, and vacuums. Boyle's colleague Robert Hooke designed what was undoubtedly one of the first air pump/vacuum chambers.

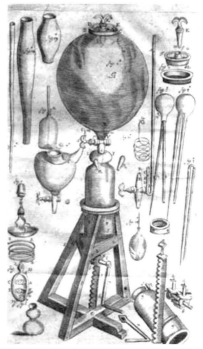

Early drawing of Robert Hooke's vacuum chamber. Photo Credit: The Robert Boyle Project.

Boyle would place bugs and other small creatures into the pump chamber and force the air out. He would then observe and record the effects of having no air on the test subjects. Obviously, there were few survivors of the airless chamber. What I want to achieve with this book is to educate, enlighten, and prevent the prepper from experiencing the same end that Boyle's unfortunate test subjects did.

Shortly thereafter, in 1715, a French aristocrat named Chevalier de Beauve successfully applied the use of a bellows air pump to his deep-sea diving suit. This was perhaps the first time an air pump was used to allow a man to survive in an adverse environment.

Another invention of note followed in the 1800s, the development of a double-action piston bellows. This type of pump moved air on both strokes for a continuous, uninterrupted supply. On an unrelated note, one of the first applications of this design was pairing it with the reed harmonica, and so was born the accordion.

It wasn't until World War II that an air pump was used in a manner that closely meets our purposes. The most useful example of an affordable air pump being used in modern times for man's survival while in a confined space comes from Zagan, Poland. For about a year, starting in the spring of 1943 through March 1944, a group of Allied prisoners of war hand-dug multiple underground escape tunnels. While in captivity and closely guarded, the soldiers not only managed to dig, but they also designed and built an air pump that fed fresh air to the men digging in the confinement of the underground tunnels.

Using whatever resources he could scrounge from his position as a prisoner of war, squad leader Robert Nelson built a highly effective air pump out of Ping-Pong paddles, hockey sticks, wood from their bunks, and other personal items, including a duffle bag. The ventilation pipe for the fresh air system was made from empty tin cans spliced together. All this took place at Stalag Luft III during the war, and the story is told in Paul Brickhill's 1950 book, *The Great Escape,* which in 1963 was made into a movie of the same name.

It is worth mentioning that the man who designed the air pumps, Robert Nelson, came to be at Stalag Luft III after losing an engine on his Vickers Wellington bomber during his 23rd combat mission. While over the deserts of North Africa, Nelson crash-landed 150 miles behind enemy lines after seeing to it that his crew had safely bailed out. He survived the crash only to face a solo 10-day walk through the desert. He was

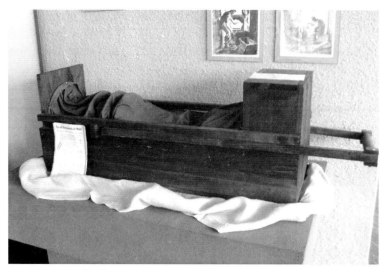

A re-creation of Robert Nelson's air pump located at the Museum of Allied Prisoners of War Martyrdom, Zagan, Poland. Photo credit: Copyright 2007, Robert Davis.

aided only once during the walk by a passing Arab who gave him water. It was further reported that he was only a mile away from Allied forces when he was captured by Rommel's troops and subsequently sent to Stalag Luft III. After his escape from there, Nelson was recaptured and returned to prison, along with several other escapees, for the duration of the war. After the war, he was released. The man was a survivor in every sense of the word!

The air-quality issues facing the men in the tunnels of Stalag Luft III are generally the same ones faced by preppers considering an underground shelter today. Basically, when discussing hand-operated air pumps, there's really nothing new. The same technology of a thousand years ago was used in Zagan, Poland, and is going to be applied by today's preppers in their underground shelters: a simple design utilizing manpower to operate. The important lesson we can take from the "Great Escape" is that a hand-operated air pump proved to be efficient enough to successfully supply air to the men digging tunnels 30 feet underground. While under stressful conditions, a group of men set on surviving were able to persevere and not only dig a tunnel but also supply enough fresh air to a confined space to support the high level of physical exertion needed to complete the task.

As new discoveries and inventions appeared to make everyday lives better, electric fans became common in households and businesses. Soon, these electric fans were recognized as the best method to move air at low pressures, and the once-common bellows became a novelty of metallurgy and wood burners. The electric fan was further developed and modified into a variety of common household items. Hair dryers, space heaters, and vacuum cleaners are essentially just modified electric fans.

Of these appliances, one stands out as being readily adaptable to our use as a shelter air pump: the vacuum cleaner, or more specifically a drum or canister vacuum cleaner. It not only moves a high volume of air, but it also filters the air. Had the prisoners of Stalag Luft III been able to get their hands on a wet/dry vac, they could have saved a lot of energy! Using the modern drum-style vacuum cleaner, the prepper can build a filtered fresh-air pump system for the home-built buried shelter that rivals some expensive ready-made air systems.

2

FRESH AIR: CAN'T LIVE WITHOUT IT

The importance of exchanging the air in your shelter-in-place location or buried bunker cannot be overemphasized. As we breathe the air in a confined space, we use up the oxygen in the air and replace it with a poisonous gas called carbon dioxide (CO_2). With every breath we take, we exhale more CO_2 and take in air that contains even less oxygen. The quality of the air in the shelter suffers in both high humidity and carbon dioxide levels, but the discomfort of the high humidity in the shelter won't be noticed much when the air runs out of oxygen. Very few dead people have complained about the humidity!

Not only will the air exchange help keep humidity levels in the shelter down, but it will also help to keep you alive and breathing more easily. The human body functions best when the blood is saturated with oxygen at a level of 92 percent or more. Our lungs do a wonderful job extracting oxygen at sea level from the outside air we breathe in, which is actually only about 21 percent oxygen. Most of what we draw into our lungs is nitrogen gas, which makes up about 78 percent of the air we breathe. As we breathe and exhale, we add carbon dioxide to the atmosphere while depleting the oxygen in the air by about

5 percent with each breath. The bottom line here is that in a closed area, the level of CO_2 will build and oxygen levels will drop, leading to a deadly situation.

There are two schools of thought when calculating the amount of breathable air in a confined space. One school focuses on the rising levels of CO_2 gas, which can kill at concentrated levels of 10 percent or more. The other is concerned with oxygen levels in the air. Since both calculations take into account that we inhale oxygen and exhale CO_2, the end results are the same. There is also some debate as to whether death comes from the inhalation of poisonous CO_2 or suffocation from the lack of oxygen, but here also the end result is the same. In this book, I focus on oxygen levels.

Fortunately, our bodies give us warning signs when we are deprived of proper levels of oxygen. Many people will show the following signs when their air supply has been diminished:

- Headache
- Sleepiness or fatigue; lethargic behavior
- Dizziness
- Blurred vision
- Confusion, uncertainty, or disorientation
- Labored breathing

In extreme conditions, people will pass out and ultimately die from suffocation unless fresh air can be brought into the shelter quickly enough.

The average adult breathes approximately 388 cubic feet of air per day. When someone is working hard and breathing heavily, this number will be greater due to the increased use of air.

For this book, my calculations and formulas are based on rounding up 388 to 400 cubic feet of air breathed per day.

Since air will indeed be one of the most precious commodities you keep in your shelter, you should consider adopting the following simple rules whenever you are inside.

- Smoking should never be permitted inside the shelter.
- Never cook any food in your sealed shelter with an open-flame heat source.
- Campfires and cookouts are for when you are outside the shelter. When the SHTF, you'll be eating cold or warm food while wearing your coats and jackets to stay warm in the shelter.
- It is important for the security and lives of everyone in the shelter to remain calm and collected at all times. A calm person will breathe less air than an excited one.
- Saving heavy exercise for when you're outdoors and keeping the shelter's door open whenever possible will also extend your oxygen supply.

Every prepper must know the size of his shelter and how much breathable air it holds. By knowing the total cubic feet less the area displaced by supplies and gear, you can roughly figure how much air is in the shelter and how long you have before the air quality begins to go bad. The Occupational Safety and Health Administration (OSHA) standard for poor-quality air in a confined space is an oxygen level of 19.5 percent or less. Anyone in a confined space with less than this *must* have ventilation or a breathing apparatus. In a small, confined space, such as a bunker or sealed shelter, it will not take long before the oxygen in the air drops to an unsafe level. The more people, the shorter the time. The only safe choice is to use a forced-ventilation system that brings fresh air into the shelter.

3

PASSIVE VENTILATION

Construction methods have varied greatly over the years. Older homes built of stone, brick, or block can be relatively tight as far as air infiltration is concerned. Older wood-framed homes are often said to "breathe" because of the many opportunities for air to pass through the exterior siding, walls, and poorly weather-stripped windows, but even newer homes using vapor barriers and top-of-the-line windows and doors can leak air. This is all too evident in the dust found over the door trim or on top of the refrigerator or ceiling fan blades.

For reasons relating more to energy efficiency than your well-being, society has been sealing up our homes from what was, at one time, natural passive ventilation. Simply put, homes today do not breathe well but still leak enough around the doors and windows to offer some level of outside air exchange. It is this air infiltration that can pose a threat when conditions outside take a turn for the worse. This is why shelter-in-place preppers must seal around doors, windows, and vents to protect occupants from outside airborne threats. Older homes may be more difficult to seal.

Buried shelters usually have no windows and few doors.

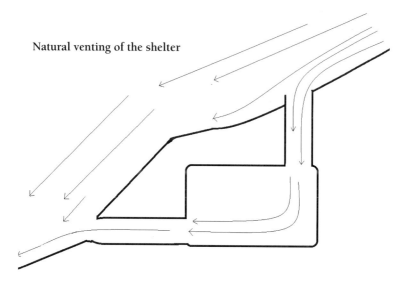

Natural venting of the shelter

What doors they do have are also usually small in size. Buried shelters are, by definition, confined spaces and must have adequate ventilation for everyone inside. Rarely does a buried shelter have any natural passive ventilation; however, under some circumstances, a buried or partially buried shelter can vent air naturally at an acceptable rate. Some locations can allow for the design of partially buried shelters to have windows and air vents, which can be covered by extended and camouflaged roofs. Adding opportunities for air to travel through the shelter can often make the difference. When placed in a remote or well-hidden area, a partially buried shelter may not need any additional ventilation when the outside air is good.

Depending on your site location and features, you may have an option for a naturally vented shelter. The best layout for this would be to have two entrances to the shelter, one at each end. When the shelter is placed on a hillside, the natural slope of the land will keep air flowing through the shelter when both doors are open. This air exchange should serve you well until such time that the doors must be closed.

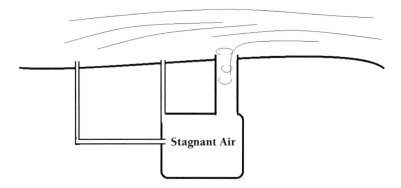

Stagnant Air

Unfortunately, not all shelters will have two or more entrances and enjoy a large, natural air exchange. Small shelters may have only one small crawl space entrance, which makes natural airflow impossible. Fully buried shelters will definitely require a bit more thought where ventilation is concerned. The forces that move air will still exist in the small shelter and will be heat related. As the bodies of the occupants heat the air in the shelter, the air will rise and vent out the top pipes and open hatches. This venting, or movement of air, creates lower air pressure in the shelter, which will draw cooler air in through another pipe. At times, this level of air exchange may be adequate, but it cannot be counted on when the shelter is locked down.

In contrast, a buried bunker with a single entrance hatch on top may never be able to develop a natural airflow. Tragically, many of the children who fall into wells (which happens all too often) die of suffocation even though the top of the well is open. A single opening will not provide adequate ventilation. If the air becomes stagnant and does not flow, its quality is depleted with every breath until the last.

A good point of reference is found in naturally occurring caves and caverns. Few spelunkers will even consider navigating caves that are not naturally well vented. These caves may or may not have a large entrance, but they will all have natural vents to the surface at several locations within the cave. An underground shelter designed and built with this in mind can attempt to duplicate the conditions that result in natural ventilation and may be able to do so without any further action. The caves that do not require an active venting system are generally very large to start with and can have any number of known and unknown natural vents, which can complicate the task of designing a passive system. Further, caves and caverns do not have doors that close and shut down the natural flow of air. Since the size of the cave or cavern is the largest contributing factor to providing breathable air to its inhabitants, and as economy-minded preppers we generally cannot build a buried shelter the size of a cavern, we need to look at the other factors. Outside weather conditions, location of entries and vents, prevailing wind conditions, and convection are all contributing factors to natural airflow.

For small buried bunkers or shelters, you'll first have to determine if a door is necessary. The shelter might have a locking door to secure it in your absence, but is this necessary when you are occupying the shelter? In some cases, a well-hidden entrance may replace the need for a securely locked door. In other instances, an open door may look inviting to critters of all sizes. These are factors you need to consider before deciding what to do in your shelter.

Shelters that are buried in hillsides and that have two large entrances will have the greatest opportunity to induce natural venting for two reasons: pressure variables and heat convection. When both doors are open, any wind outside the shelter will create a low-pressure area at the door opening and can trigger air movement from inside the shelter. Air moves from high-pressure to low-pressure areas. Low-pressure air is relatively cooler than high-pressure air. Drops in pressure react similarly to drops in heat.

Air temperature differences can also trigger natural ventilation when the outside air is colder than the air inside the shelter and will "sink" into a top shelter entrance, moving the air through your vents. The same happens when heat from your body rises and causes air movement.

Caves in North America generally maintain a year-round air temperature that is relative to the soil temperature in their regions. East Coast caves average about 52 degrees Fahrenheit (F), while caves in the warmer Southwest desert average about 62 degrees. It can be expected that shelters buried in various areas will have similar year-round constants inside the shelter as caves do since the temperature of the surrounding earth and soil influences the air temperature.

It should also be noted that the buried shelter can produce fog, just as a cave can under certain conditions. When the air inside the shelter is warmer and wetter than the cold, dry air outside, a light fog can develop at the entrance. For some this may be of no concern; however, hunters and woodsmen will often look for small patches of fog on cold mornings to identify areas where game animals bed down and for caves or dens where big game might be found.

All said, finding a cave with natural ventilation might prove to be an easier task than building a passively vented buried shelter that you can keep well hidden at the same time. Therefore, nearly all buried shelters will require some type of active ventilation system. *This is especially true when airborne threats exist!*

ACTIVE
VENTILATION

The only sure way to know that breathable air is getting into your shelter is to pump it there yourself. Having a positive flow of air from outside the shelter into the living area will displace trapped and stagnant air by driving it out of the passive exhaust pipes or exhaust ports you've installed. By pumping air into your shelter, you are creating a slightly higher pressure (overpressure) inside the shelter, which will start the inside air flowing to the closest low-pressure area. This low-pressure area is found at the passive air exhaust pipes typically installed near the floor level of the buried bunker or at a doorway to an adjoining room when sheltering in place.

Having overpressure inside the shelter is the preferred condition. In contrast, a system that pumps air out of the shelter would find you in an area with a slightly lower pressure than outside (underpressure). In a sense, you'd be living in a vacuum, and the higher-pressure air outside the shelter would seek a way in through any means possible, including your passive exhaust pipes. As long as the air pump is in operation, you will have air that is as fresh as what is outside and above your shelter.

Under the adverse conditions that would drive a prepper to the shelter, there are only two means to provide power for the air pump: electricity and manpower. Whether it's an electric or a hand-operated air pump, everyone in your shelter will need to be aware of how it functions and take part in monitoring your active ventilation system. You're all in this together. Educate everyone about the signs and symptoms associated with low oxygen levels in the air and what to do about it. With everyone informed and ready to take an active role in keeping fresh air flowing into the shelter, you can survive.

5

SHELTER-IN-PLACE EMERGENCY AIR MANAGEMENT

In the event of an attack against the United States that utilizes nuclear, radiological, or biological weapons, many citizens will be forced to protect themselves by sheltering in place—simply put, sheltering indoors wherever they happen to be when the event occurs. Of the many potential types of health concerns and threats to life such attacks would pose, inhaling contaminated airborne particles is just one. Remaining safe from airborne contaminants while in the affected region will require those who are sheltering in place to seal themselves indoors. This discussion focuses on effective air management for those citizens who follow Federal Emergency Management Agency (FEMA) suggestions and seal themselves inside a room, house, or office using duct tape, plastic sheeting, and other materials. There are other necessary actions that will be required under these circumstances, but these are not covered here in great depth. Without an air supply, all other preparations will become moot in a very short time.

Shortly after the events of September 11, 2001, additional terrorist attacks were attempted or threatened against the United States. One of these threats used an airborne biological weapon known as anthrax. Since that time, FEMA has identified additional potential threats against the public that include "dirty bombs" (radioactive material dispersed using an explosive device that scatters radioactive materials in a wide area), "suitcase nuclear devices," and such biological weapons as engineered viruses. All these types of threats and attacks contaminate the air with either radioactive or poisonous dust particles that lead to either serious health problems or death if inhaled.

The practice of sheltering in place is designed to protect people in the affected areas by quickly finding shelter and sealing off a building or room from the contaminated air outside. This is accomplished by using duct tape and plastic sheeting to seal off points of air infiltration in the shelter structure. FEMA has published guidelines for the use of duct tape and plastic sheeting by the general public as protection but has yet (as of this writing) to offer instructions on how to be relatively safe in allowing fresh breathable air into the sealed shelter in order to replace the oxygen-depleted air being breathed in the confined space. Instead FEMA has advised citizens who are sheltering in place to listen to news reports for information and further instructions. This is problematic, since there could potentially be many circumstances during a national attack that could delay or prevent the timely broadcast of information to the general public.

A power-grid failure or an electromagnetic pulse (EMP) event in the immediate area of a nuclear strike could easily delay vital information from getting to citizens who are downwind and sheltering in place in a yet to be affected fallout zone. Unfortunately, even in this information age, it can take a lot of time for the first responders on the ground to access the situation and report back through the chain of command and then broadcast the alert. Many people will seek shelter at the first hint of such an event by the media without waiting for confirmation.

The logical question for the prepper to ask next is, "So, how much air do I have?" Several variables determine the answer to this question. In fact, it can only be answered by nailing down these variables to an acceptable fixed state or condition.

Roughly speaking, an example of how much breathable air is contained in what might be considered a common-sized, sealed "shelter-in-place" location is to consider the average home's eat-in kitchen. If the overall size of the room is 10 feet wide by 16 feet in length with an 8-foot high ceiling, the room would contain 1,280 cubic feet of air if it were empty. A rough calculation must be made to deduct the volume of air displaced by everything in the room, including the people. For our example, we'll say that the furniture, supplies, and people displace approximately 280 cubic feet. This leaves 1,000 cubic feet of air in the room. The average person when at rest breathes about 400 cubic feet of air in a 24-hour period.

If the above room were to be sealed, you might believe that the person would have over two and a half days of breathable air in the room before he would have to replenish it. *This would be a deadly mistake!*

In the above example, the sealed room with one person breathing and depleting the oxygen only has about 12 hours before the air reaches the unsafe level of 19.5 percent, not two and a half days! This allows for one hour of breathable air for every 80 cubic feet of air in the shelter per person: (total cubic

Shelter Safety for Sealed Rooms

Ten square feet of floor space per person will provide sufficient air to prevent carbon dioxide build-up for up to five hours, assuming a normal breathing rate while resting.

However, local officials are unlikely to recommend the public shelter in a sealed room for more than 2-3 hours because the effectiveness of such sheltering diminishes with time as the contaminated outside air gradually seeps into the shelter. At this point, evacuation from the area is the better protective action to take.

Also you should ventilate the shelter when the emergency has passed to avoid breathing contaminated air still inside the shelter.

FEMA *Technological Hazards 3.1.*

feet of shelter air) divided by (80) = total hours of breathable air for one person.

The FEMA publication *Technological Hazards Part 3.1* comes to the same conclusion but words it a bit differently: OSHA has set guidelines that identify any confined area with less than 19.5-percent oxygen in the air as being unsafe for anyone without a breathing apparatus. It is clear that a room sealed with duct tape and plastic sheeting can cross this dangerous threshold in a very short time. In reality, the air we breathe contains about 21-percent oxygen. With each breath our lungs extract oxygen from the air, and we exhale air with about a 16-percent oxygen content. This depletion continues with each breath and lowers the overall 21-percent oxygen we started with, unless there is a new supply of fresh air.

Yet, even with 12 hours of breathable air in the room, action must be taken *before* the oxygen levels get this low. Do not test your limits. At the 19.5-percent level, some people may start to have diminished consciousness or even pass out.

Going back to the example above, if there were two people in the same sealed room, the amount of time before the room was depleted of breathable air would be cut in half, to just six hours. If a family of four were in the shelter, their time would drop to about three hours before they found themselves in a dangerous environment. A group of 12 coworkers in a sealed break room of the same size would have less than an hour before the air reached the dangerous level. These people could not afford to wait even an hour for the critical information needed to survive.

Even with the best planning, during a national emergency it is unlikely that sensitive air-quality monitors will be deployed, placed online, and able to report the level of airborne threats to the public in less than two hours. Yet in that same amount of time, there will be groups of people sheltering in place who have already run out of oxygen. Without a source of breathable air, their choice would be to either breathe the outside air and expose themselves to the threat or insulate themselves from the outside threat and suffocate in their shelters.

The issue has a simple, two-part solution. First, awareness must be elevated to the point that preppers understand the limits of their sheltering location and can safely calculate how much time they have before their shelter must be ventilated. Second, the outside air must be filtered to a level that restricts the contaminated particles from entering the shelter's air supply when replenishment is needed.

It is highly unlikely that the countless structures used by citizens to shelter in place will have expensive air cleaners and filters to accomplish this, but they all may indeed have an item that can serve them in that time of crisis: the vacuum cleaner. A vacuum cleaner with a high-efficiency particulate air (HEPA) filter might be the single-most important item needed in the event of a nuclear or biological emergency. Everyone needs to have one ready with the shelter-in-place supplies.

Wherever electric power is available, using your drum vacuum cleaner (along with a HEPA filter) as a fresh air pump will allow you to filter the contaminated particles from the air and safely ventilate the sealed shelter when needed.

What many consumers don't know or have lost sight of is that the HEPA filter was originally developed in the 1940s by the U.S. Atomic Energy Commission and was used during the Manhattan Project to protect scientists and workers from breathing radioactive dust particles in the workplace. By definition, it's not a HEPA filter if it doesn't meet the standard of filtering 99.97 percent of all particles .3 microns or larger. As a side note, the HEPA filter also removed a wide variety of troublesome airborne particles, such as allergens, pollen, bacteria, and cat dander, to name just a few. Most consumer-targeted ads fail to mention nuclear fallout and some pandemic threats. Go figure.

Today, many homes and businesses have vacuum cleaners with HEPA filters that can be put to use in an emergency to filter the breathing air during the aftermath of a nuclear, dirty bomb, anthrax, or other biological weapon attack. Research into this matter has determined that while any vacuum with the appropriate HEPA filter can be placed into service as an

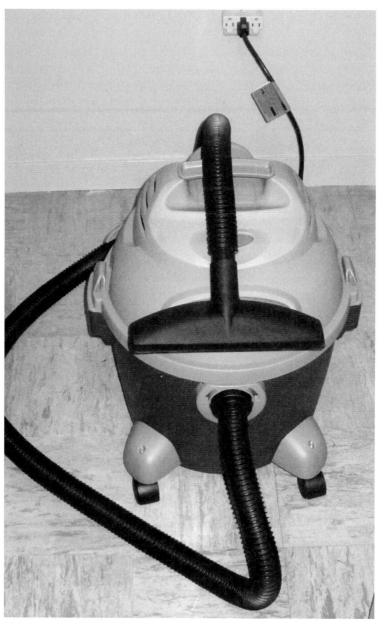

This common household tool could make the difference between your surviving a nuclear/biological attack and failing to do so.

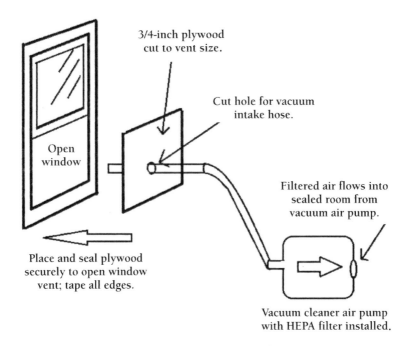

3/4-inch plywood
cut to vent size.

Cut hole for vacuum
intake hose.

Open
window

Filtered air flows into
sealed room from
vacuum air pump.

Place and seal plywood
securely to open window
vent; tape all edges.

Vacuum cleaner air pump
with HEPA filter installed.

air pump and filter during an emergency, there are good reasons for those who plan ahead to have a dedicated unit, along
with spares.

First, a new unit and an unused HEPA filter will offer the
longest possible service life and allow the prepper to shelter in
place longer. Used vacuums will be dirty and the filter most
likely clogged with dust, dirt, lint, and hair. Since time will be of
the essence, you will not want to stop to clean your old vacuum
cleaner and filter. Additionally, common household lint, hair, and
dirt are typically larger than many potentially hazardous dusts
you hope to filter. Just one hair lodged between the filter and the
vacuum head can allow unwanted outside-air infiltration.

Second, while it is true that some HEPA filters can be

cleaned and used repeatedly, they are fragile and can be damaged easily in the cleaning process. A damaged filter can allow dangerous particles to infiltrate your shelter.

Third, if you find that you are indeed in a heavily contaminated area, your vacuum cleaner will be filled with contaminated dust by the end of your stay in the shelter. The vacuum cannot be safely opened and serviced and, therefore, should remain sealed with the intake and exhaust openings closed off. The vacuum itself is the containment unit for whatever hazardous particles it happens to collect and should be properly disposed of when full and replaced with a new unit.

Under these emergency circumstances in which vacuum cleaners are considered to be disposable containment units, the best vacuum to use is one with the largest surface area of HEPA filter at the lowest cost. A $500 vacuum will not necessarily work any better than a $100 one. In fact, many "upright" consumer vacuums that use HEPA filters have a relatively small filter that will fill with contaminants long before larger filters would under similar conditions. The most cost-effective unit available today that has both a HEPA filter with a large surface area and a relatively low cost is the wet/dry style drum vacuum. Its features and accessories are also compatible for use as suggested here.

Use caution in choosing space for your shelter-in-place location. There are threat-specific factors to consider. In a nuclear fallout situation, a basement or area that offers a large mass of earth or concrete to shield you from outside threats offers better protection than the ground level of a wood-framed house. Additionally, your shelter-in-place room should not be more than 200 square feet. This size restriction is based on the vacuum's ability to maintain an overpressure strong enough to force out the stale air when the system is running.

By following the instructions below, anyone with a vacuum cleaner and a HEPA filter has a fighting chance to survive if caught in a region directly affected by any of these types of emergencies. These instructions will guide you step-by-step in how to properly seal and install a vacuum/air filter pump.

1. Once you have your vacuum unit and HEPA filter, install the filter to ensure that there is no blow-by or bypass of air around the filter. All air must travel through the filter before it enters your shelter. To do this you must first follow the instructions for proper filter installation, being certain that the filter and power head are clean and the filter is seated tightly to the power head of the vacuum unit.

2. Using either metal or duct tape, cover all seams between the filter and the power head, and the filter and the filter retainer end cap. Use short, small pieces of tape and press firmly as you go around the seams. This is a critical point! Inspect carefully and confirm a positive seal. Add tape anywhere the seal looks questionable. *Note:* Some vacuums will come from the manufacturer with a reusable disk filter and mounting ring or a filter cover that acts as a pre-filter to the HEPA cartridge. This type of pre-filter can be placed over the HEPA cartridge and secured with a large rubber band or a length of string or shoelace. Extra caution must be used when placing the pre-filter over the taped areas to be certain the seal is not broken. Do not use the rigid plastic mounting ring supplied by the manufacturer, which can undo your tape job in short order.

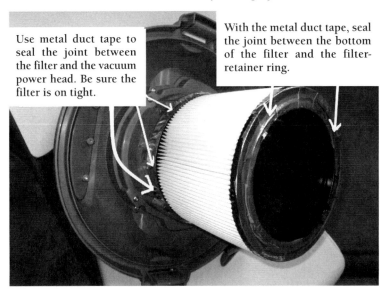

Use metal duct tape to seal the joint between the filter and the vacuum power head. Be sure the filter is on tight.

With the metal duct tape, seal the joint between the bottom of the filter and the filter-retainer ring.

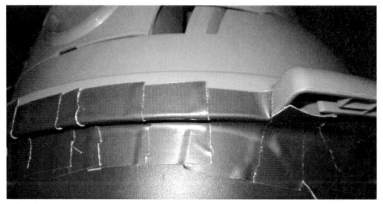

After being certain that the power head is properly latched, use small pieces of duct tape to seal the joint between the head and the tank. Inspect to be sure all gaps are sealed.

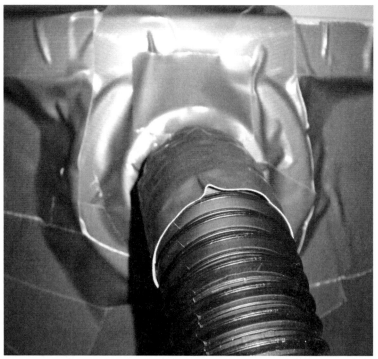

Attach the hose to the intake port of the unit and, using duct tape, seal the joints and seams where the hose and fittings meet the unit.

3. Once the filter is installed and the seams are sealed with duct tape, place the power head back on the tank assembly and latch it in place.
4. Using duct tape, completely seal the seam between the power head and tank assembly, pressing firmly as you go around the entire unit.
5. Attach the hose to the intake port of the unit and, using duct tape, seal the joints and seams where the hose and fittings meet the unit.
6. Setting the unit aside for now, choose a window for your air source. If you are familiar with the structure you are sheltering in, choose a window on the side of the building that you know to have the least amount of dust. Otherwise, take a guess at it. You don't want your filter filling with local dust before the threat arrives. Open the window and storm window (if any). Tape the sash in the open position to be certain it will not close. Clean the area around the window opening. The window screen may be left closed to keep large debris and insects out.
7. Lay out a piece of plastic sheeting large enough to cover the open vent of your window. Use the floor or other flat surface as a workspace (see below).

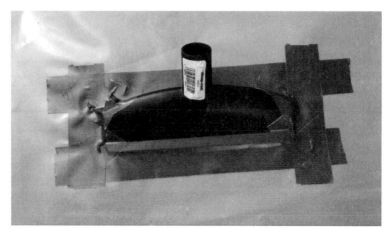

8. Using duct tape, tape the vacuum's 10-inch combination floor nozzle flat to the center of the plastic sheeting. It should be carefully sealed all the way around the nozzle.

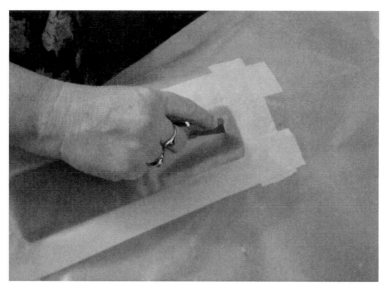

9. Carefully turn the plastic sheeting over with the now plastic-covered side of the nozzle intake facing you. Use a razor knife or pair of scissors to cut a slit down the center of the nozzle opening in the plastic sheeting.

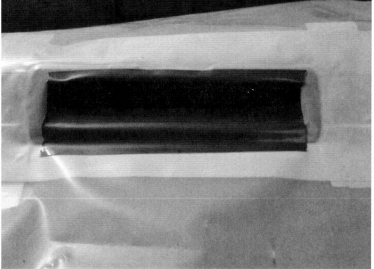

10. Trim the ends of your first cut, both up and down, so the plastic will now fold neatly into the vacuum nozzle opening (top). Secure these loose ends using duct tape to the inside of the nozzle (bottom).

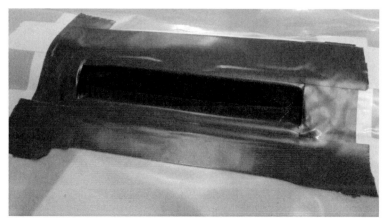

11. Using more duct tape, frame the back side of the plastic sheeting at the same locations you did on the other side for added support.

12. If available, tape a pre-filter or a piece of cotton T-shirt over the open end of the vacuum nozzle to keep heavy dirt and insects out of your filter. Tape all the way around the pre-filter, being careful not to block or tape over the nozzle opening. The pre-filter should cover the opening, not the tape!

Use duct tape to seal the joint between the hose and nozzle.

13. Apply plastic sheeting with duct tape to seal the window, following FEMA instructions, and then add the cut piece to your air-source window. Be sure that the outside of your sheeting (the side with the pre-filter) is open to the outdoors. It is best to have it inside your window screen yet outside the sealed plastic sheeting. The window screen is a welcome added protection.

14. Bring the vacuum unit over to the air-source window and attach the intake hose to the nozzle, which is now taped to the plastic sheeting. Use duct tape to seal the joint at the hose and nozzle to prevent any air infiltration.

15. Do your air-supply calculations to determine how much breathable air you have in your sealed shelter. You must know this to determine how long you can safely breathe before turning on the vacuum/filtered air pump. The vacuum is not made for continuous use. It must be turned on and al-

HOW TO CALCULATE OXYGEN NEEDS FOR ROOMS

Length x Width x Height (in feet)

$$\frac{}{} = \boxed{\text{Total cubic feet in room}}$$

Deduct cubic feet volume
of everything in the room.

Imagine everything in the room being in one square
stack, including all the people. How big is the pile?

Length x Width x Height (in feet)

$$\frac{}{} = \boxed{\text{Total cubic feet of stuff}}$$

Total cubic feet of room
Minus (-) total cubic feet of stuff
Equals (=) total cubic feet of air in room

This room has _____ total cubic feet of air.

TIME CALCULATIONS FOR BREATHABLE AIR

In a sealed room, allow for one hour of breathable air per person for every 80 total cubic feet of air in the shelter.

Total cubic feet of air divided by (÷)

Number of people in shelter times (x) 80

Equals (=)

Number of hours before vacuum must be used

Total cubic feet of air in your shelter

Number of people in shelter

x 80 =

Number of hours before room runs out of breathable air

lowed to run for at least 15 minutes (for our example room) every time the room's oxygen level gets low. Use the CFM rating of the vacuum to determine how long it needs to run for the size of your sealed shelter, but in most cases 15 minutes will be plenty of time to run the unit.

16. Determine the location of your air exhaust port. Once the vacuum is turned on, the stale air needs an exit hole to an adjoining room. Lifting the tape at the bottom of an interior doorway and allowing air to exit will work fine. The opening should be about one square foot in size. The overpressure (increased pressure) created by the vacuum filling the shelter with fresh air will be greater than the pressure in the adjoining room and, therefore, will force air out the opening. Always open the exhaust port *after* the vacuum is turned on and close the port *before* it is turned off! Have extra tape available to reseal the opening if necessary.

17. Manage your air and time by refreshing the shelter's air before the air becomes heavy with CO_2 and is oxygen depleted. Listen to news reports for further information or instructions about the threat.

Note: If your group is too large for a 200-square-foot room and there is only one vacuum cleaner and HEPA filter available, there is a possible alternative. Providing that there are two adjoining rooms that both have exterior windows and a suitable exhaust port available, and there is an extra vacuum nozzle to tape to the extra room's exterior window, the vacuum can be shared between the two rooms.

Follow the earlier precautions and seal the nozzle inlet immediately after removing the vacuum hose. Extra care should be taken not to disturb the plastic sheeting or pull it off the window. Open the plastic sheeting between the two rooms long enough to pass the vacuum back and forth. Another alternative would be to purchase additional hose in order to extend the vacuum's fresh air exhaust into the adjoining room by passing just the hose under the sheeting.

Any drum-style vacuum cleaner that has a HEPA filter

available can be easily modified for this purpose, but for the practical demonstration I have chosen a common and inexpensive 6-gallon size. It is a nationally recognized brand that I have owned several different models of over the years, and they have never let me down. It is rated to move 130 cubic feet of air per minute, and it was advertised as being quieter than other vacuums. It was also the least-expensive model that has an available HEPA filter upgrade. After testing for noise level, I found that it certainly isn't quiet, yet it doesn't scream like some other vacuums I've used in the past. The vacuum unit cost me about $50 at a local big-box lumberyard. The HEPA filter was an additional $40 online.

This smaller model, 130 cubic feet per minute (CFM), was also chosen for use in smaller-sized shelters. Larger and more powerful vacuums, up to 200 CFM, can cost up to $400 and might be more suitable for larger shelters that protect more people or might last longer than the less expensive models.

One FEMA publication that details recommendations for the construction of safe rooms suggests that all sealed shelters having a filtered-air-pump system maintain an overpressure. The above chart from that publication compares shelters of different construction materials and levels of "air-tightness" in being sealed for air infiltration. Preppers will have to realistically rate their shelter's "air-tightness" level and decide for themselves how it compares to this chart.

Older homes that have not been improved with vapor barriers and sealing caulks are not very tight while many newer homes built to higher energy standards are much better sealed. As mentioned previously, all windows, no matter how expensive, will leak some air. It is impossible to have a window with any moving vent that does not leak some amount of air. Everyone must seal all windows in the shelter.

The chart on the next page should be referred to when purchasing a vacuum for use in this manner. The CFM flow rating of the vacuum should be considered the basis for the maximum size of your sealed shelter. A vacuum rated at 130 CFM, in theory, should be able to service a 130-square-foot shelter inside

Construction Type	cfm per square foot of floor area
Very tight: 26-inch thick concrete walls and roof with no windows	0.04
Tight: 12-inch thick concrete or block walls and roof with tight windows and multiple, sealed penetrations	0.20
Typical: 12-inch thick concrete or block walls with gypsum wall board ceilings or composition roof and multiple, sealed penetrations	0.50
Loose: Wood-frame construction without special sealing measures	1.00

FEMA Table 3.2. Note the varying levels of air leakage in the various types of construction materials.

an older wood-framed house. The same unit might be able to service a larger room in a tightly sealed concrete structure. These factors are left to the judgment of the prepper.

The vacuum cleaner air pump detailed here can be used by anyone who is caught in a region for which sheltering in place has been recommended. Even someone caught away from home can use this knowledge and join others in that area in putting together a system so they all can breathe safely.

Today, there are many people who take chemical and nuclear threats seriously and identify themselves as preppers. As such, they are always looking for the best methods for preparing for whatever threats they believe to be real and present dangers. There is an improvement to the system worth mentioning for those preppers who recognize any of the threats mentioned here and are actively taking steps in planning for them by purchasing a wet/dry vacuum along with a HEPA filter to keep as a dedicated unit.

It shouldn't come as much of a surprise to learn that there are several industries that are extremely concerned with filtering large volumes of air in order to remove airborne threats. One of them, in particular, deals with sealed structures that are quite large and hold a large volume of air. Commercial organic growers all over the country commonly use outdoor-rated

HEPA filters at the air-intake pipe to their greenhouses to protect their organic crops from airborne threats such as GMO pollens, bacteria, viruses, insects, and other threats commonly found floating in the air.

These HEPA filters are made for common-sized pipes and can be used just as easily by preppers who plan ahead. In fact, by using this type of HEPA outdoor pre-filter with the system detailed in this book, the shelter-in-place prepper now has a two-stage HEPA system, offering twice the protection and greatly reducing the potential hazard of having the containment unit in the shelter.

In planning ahead, outside the window in the designated shelter room, a fixed pipe with the HEPA filter can be attached to the exterior wall. When the time to shelter in place arrives, the same vacuum cleaner system detailed above would be installed, but it would be connected directly to the bottom of the pipe along the exterior wall. Tape and sheeting can be used to seal around the vacuum's flexible hose that passes through the window.

The drawing on the facing page details how the double HEPA filter system might be used when you have planned ahead.

By following the instructions contained in this book, average citizens can gain a means to filter air contaminated with airborne particulate threats, and shelter in place using the FEMA guidelines and suggestions. Sealing a room with duct tape and plastic sheeting in your home or at your office can now be done safely. Using this system will give those people having to shelter in place the needed air to breathe while listening for updates to the situation outside.

Note: It is important to note that Shop Vac and the other vacuum cleaner manufacturers did not design their vacuum cleaners to be used for shelter air filtration. The author's choice is what he believes to be the best unit adaptable for this purpose and in no way should imply or suggest that manufacturers endorse the use or modification of their products for use in this manner. You may well void your warranty, but you just may save your family. The choice is yours to make.

DOUBLE HEPA FILTER PROTECTION

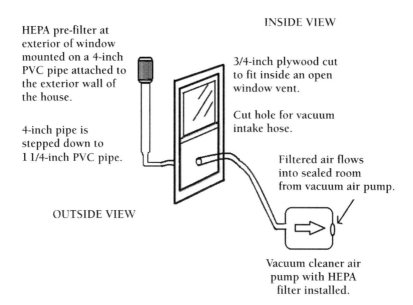

HEPA pre-filter at exterior of window mounted on a 4-inch PVC pipe attached to the exterior wall of the house.

4-inch pipe is stepped down to 1 1/4-inch PVC pipe.

OUTSIDE VIEW

INSIDE VIEW

3/4-inch plywood cut to fit inside an open window vent.

Cut hole for vacuum intake hose.

Filtered air flows into sealed room from vacuum air pump.

Vacuum cleaner air pump with HEPA filter installed.

6

POWERING
YOUR PUMPS

Shelter-in-place preppers will either be powering their vacuum cleaner air pumps with on-grid power or home generators. If the power grid fails and the only source for power is a generator, you must ration fuel and use it only when your shelter requires ventilation. Air must be your first priority!

Where buried bunkers are concerned, there are a number of options for providing power for the air pumps. The easiest option is to just run a hidden extension cord underground to the nearest outbuilding and either plug it in or hardwire it to your electric grid. If you have power available at your shelter's building site, this option would make the most sense for keeping your shelter ready for any situation that doesn't include a power failure. If the power grid goes down, the supply of breathable air in the sealed shelter will be limited at best. You will need an alternative source of power to keep your electric-powered air pumps operating. All said, the electric-powered vacuum air pump is still the best option.

Another consideration is that the threat is nuclear in nature and the power grid fails due to the effects of an electromagnetic pulse (EMP). The potential of fallout would send you to the bunker, but without an alternative power source you'd be in trouble. A societal breakdown might place a limit on the total gallons of fuel you have to run your generator and, therefore, end the use of your air pump when the fuel runs out.

A dedicated solar panel with a battery bank is one alternative, but it has a couple of negatives that, depending on your circumstances, may be deal breakers. The first is that these small solar panel power grids can crash after just a few days without sunshine. Second, solar panels cannot be hidden from view without interfering with their function. Either of these situations could make even a sunny day gloomy by giving away your position when the panels act like giant signal mirrors, reflecting the sun to passing aircraft. Solar panels have a way of saying to the general public, "Hey! Look over here!"

One option would be to fence and secure your solar panels inside a small compound, positioning them where they can collect the sunshine without drawing attention to your shelter's location. I think this would be a difficult task, but even if you were successful in camouflaging your shelter from the solar panel array's compound, you would still be facing the need for a gas- or diesel-powered generator to fill in when the cloudy days persist.

Generators bring their own set of problems to the mix. Adding a noisy generator can quickly bring unwanted attention to your shelter's location and greatly diminish your security. Starting off with a quiet generator would be a good start, but the best way to both quiet and hide a generator is to bury it in a bunker of its own.

One of the quietest gasoline-powered generators on the market today is the Honda EU2000i, which was designed for use in RV parks and campgrounds. At this writing, $1,500 about covers the generator, remote starter, and extended-run gas tank. Digging a simple, earth-sided bunker with a timber and plywood roof would be more than enough to put the generator in operation for electric fans and other electrical appliances in your buried shelter. The only other consideration would be that gas engines require air to run. Your generator's buried shelter will require both an air intake pipe with a pump and a passive exhaust pipe. The bathroom fan air pump detailed later in this book would be more than adequate for supplying air to a buried generator and could also be powered by the generator.

Be certain to place your generator bunker far enough away from your buried shelter that the exhaust (carbon monoxide or carbon dioxide gas) from the engine does not concentrate near your shelter's air intake pipe.

All said, having an electric ventilation system installed in your underground shelter should be considered a must, but a hand-operated secondary system should also be installed as the emergency backup. A well-made hand pump will not fail during a solar flare or an EMP event, nor will it require a generator that will make a lot of noise and potentially expose your presence to the world. The hand-operated air pump can help keep you in your shelter when that's where you most need to be.

7

HOW TO VENTILATE
AND PLUMB YOUR
BUNKER FOR AIR

The time to start thinking about your shelter's ventilation system is when you first choose your location. The fully buried shelter will rely entirely on an air pump of some type and several runs of pipe or conduit to keep safe levels of oxygen in the shelter. This opens the door to several other concerns. Just as the design of the shelter must take into consideration the weight of the earth above it, so must your air system's supply pipes. As described in the previous chapter, the men of Stalag Luft III were able to splice together used tin cans and create a long run of metal pipe to transport the air provided by their double-action pump to the men working in the tunnel. However, their tin can pipe ran from their barracks and through their underground tunnel and was not subject to the direct weight of the earth above. Various types of pipe can be used, but when purchasing new pipe the best choice is schedule 40 PVC pipe. If one of your air pipes must run shallow or under a road or driveway, the thicker-walled schedule 80 might be needed.

Schedule 40 plumbing pipe is found at any big-box home center in a variety of sizes and your choice of black or white. It is a good choice to use for air, since it will hold up to the weight and pressures the surrounding earth and dirt exert on

PLUMBING THE BURIED SHELTER

Note: Both intake and exhaust pipes should be laid so none of the pipes are exposed to the outside and they are in a direct line to the bunker itself. Do not provide an attacker a tunnel through which to shoot at you! All pipes should run through at least 3 feet of packed earth and then turn 90 degrees before heading to the surface.

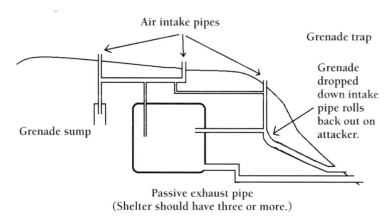

Air intake pipes

Grenade trap

Grenade dropped down intake pipe rolls back out on attacker.

Grenade sump

Passive exhaust pipe
(Shelter should have three or more.)

it. Some other lighter-grade pipes could collapse when buried and would be useless in providing you with breathable air.

Depending on your circumstances, either a 3- or 4-inch PVC schedule 40 pipe can be used for the passive exhaust pipes. Every buried shelter should have several passive exhaust pipes located at both upper and lower levels. Each air pump system may use a different diameter intake pipe, depending on the design. The choice will be yours to make once you put together your air pump system.

It should be noted that both the 3- and 4-inch pipes are large enough to allow a smoke bomb or grenade to be dropped down into the shelter. Plan your plumbing accordingly if you think your shelter may be attacked. It should be further noted that any size pipe can allow water or fluids to flow down and flood your shelter or be ignited if flammable. Take extra precautions if you think this is a potential threat to your shelter.

A well-planned ventilation system will include redundancies to ensure the positive flow of quality air into the shelter. This is done by having two or more intake pipes, along with

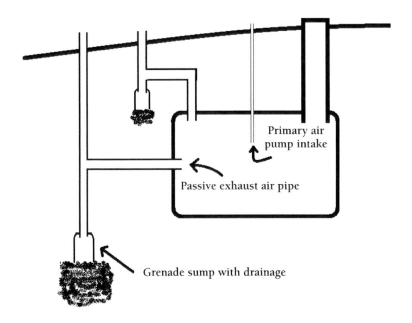

Primary air
pump intake

Passive exhaust air pipe

Grenade sump with drainage

two or more exhaust pipes. All the pipes should surface at different locations that are well concealed from the view of anyone passing through the area. It is advisable to include a grenade sump in all pipes 3 inches or greater in diameter, both intake and exhaust, when they run vertically to the shelter. If you believe there is the threat of having fluids poured down any of your vent pipes, include a sump to catch and drain the fluids before they enter your shelter.

Take extra care to be certain that none of the exposed pipes can be used as a tunnel to shoot through and pepper a prepper inside the shelter. All pipes should surface as far away from the shelter as you can reasonably afford and incorporate at least one 90-degree turn. Grenade sumps and traps should be located where there is a minimum of 3 feet of hard-packed earth or solid concrete between the trap and the shelter. As an additional precaution, dig a separate trench for any power or communication wiring and, if possible, keep it completely buried to its source. Generators can be buried in their own box shelter nearby, as can any water storage tanks.

Whenever conditions allow, both the air-intake and passive exhaust pipes at the ground surface level should be camouflaged from view. The pipes themselves should be screened to prevent insects and small critters from entering the pipe and should have some form of rain cap over the top to keep rainwater out. The length of pipe exposed above ground level should be only enough to ensure that, in a heavy rain, a flash flood doesn't swamp your shelter. If dust is an issue in your area, look for ways to keep it from blowing toward your intake pipes.

It is common to see shelters with all of the wiring, air, and water conduits exiting at the main entrance. This will allow anyone who discovers the main hatch to have access to your life-supporting plumbing and electricity. Aboveground generators with extension cords leading into the woods before disappearing into the ground can be a dead giveaway, too. Keeping all your supply lines separate and well concealed can keep you inside your shelter longer when you must be inside to be safe.

When using a buried gasoline- or diesel-powered generator, an outside air source and exhaust pipe will be needed. Be certain to locate these far enough away from your shelter's air intake pipes so as to not interfere with the quality of air you bring into your shelter. Most gases used in warfare, by design, will typically remain concentrated at levels below 30 feet off the ground in order to have the most effect on ground troops. This could cause an issue for the prepper's air intake. If this type of attack is anticipated, an intake pipe that draws on air 30 feet or higher above ground level is the only safe choice. Keeping a 30-foot aboveground air-intake pipe concealed is not as difficult as you might think. First, find the nearest 30-foot structure or make one.

PVC air intake pipes look like typical plumbing vent pipes. As such, they would be unnoticed when routed against or inside a building's wall and through the roof for about a foot. PVC pipes are also similar to plastic conduit pipes and not looked at twice alongside an antenna tower supporting a TV antenna or dish. In the alternative, when given enough time to plan, a black PVC air-intake pipe can be run next to a tree and concealed with honeysuckle or other non-poisonous vines. Running your intake pipe to higher ground is still another way to beat a gas attack on your site.

Note: Be sure to use PVC cement at all joints and allow the pipe cement to cure and dry before drawing any air through the pipes. A properly sealed pipe joint will not allow groundwater to seep into your air pipe.

A NOTE ABOUT BLAST VALVES

Blast valves are used on many commercially available air-ventilation systems to seal the bunker off from a rapidly changing environment outside. A rapid and significant increase or decrease in the outside air pressure can either force unwanted contaminated air inside your bunker or suck all your breathing air right out. The blast valve is a pressure-sensitive device that closes when these changes occur and seals off the bunker until the balance of pressure stabilizes.

The concern here again is the cost of these valves, which must be installed on all intake and exhaust pipes used in your buried bunker. For many, this is not going to be affordable; however, the truth of the matter is that, even for those folks who can afford a blast valve for each air pipe, it won't do them any good unless they are in their buried shelter with the doors closed and located within the outer fringe of ground zero during a nuclear strike or extinction level event (ELE), such as a killer asteroid. Without an early warning, the blast valve for those in the above-described areas will be meaningless.

Blast valves are not necessary for protection from radioactive fallout brought into regions with the weather or for protection from other airborne particulate threats.

8

AIR MANAGEMENT
FOR THE
HOME-BUILT
BUNKER

Whether you are building your own buried shelter or modifying an existing underground structure, you can save thousands of dollars and perhaps many lives by using an ordinary everyday drum vacuum cleaner along with upgraded filters as your primary air pump.

Just as it was detailed earlier for shelter-in-place locations, the drum-type vacuum cleaner will readily adapt to service as a buried-bunker air pump. Here, too, by using a model that has a HEPA filter available, you can add the necessary protection you'll need when retreating from nuclear or dirty bomb fallout, anthrax threats, and other biological attacks. The first part of the instructions found in Chapter 5 relating to how the vacuum cleaner and HEPA filter are sealed must be followed for any vacuum unit used in this manner.

With the additional plumbing detailed in this chapter, the home-built bunker can gain some tactical security by routing the flow of your vacuum air pump to allow it to be reversed and to expel or blow out any smoke or gases passively or intentionally vented into the shelter from the outside. Under this emergency circumstance when the flow is reversed, fresh air may be found where the passive exhaust pipe meets the shel-

ter. It should be noted that, while sheltering in place, the underpressure created by reversing the flow will draw air from any weak points in the room's seals and should only be continued long enough to clear the shelter.

The plans that follow are perhaps the least expensive route a prepper can take to ensure that everyone in the buried bunker is able to breathe fresh air. When a vacuum cleaner is purchased new for this purpose, along with a HEPA filter, and is not used in the general cleaning of the bunker, it should have a long service life and be ready when the SHTF. Of course, this air pump also requires a supply of electricity from either the power grid or a local generator.

The following drawings detail how to plumb your vacuum air pump inside your shelter. The plumbing for this system is isolated and not connected to any other of the shelter's venting pipes. This design will also require passive exhaust vent pipes to be installed in the shelter in order for stale air to exit as your vacuum air pump brings fresh air in.

PVC PIPE DETAIL FOR VACUUM/AIR PUMP SYSTEM WITH EMERGENCY EXHAUST ABILITY

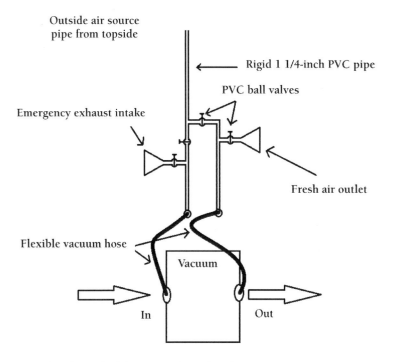

It is recommended that at some point in your PVC intake line, a T or Y fitting be used to offer an alternative intake. This option can further be improved with a valve located inside the shelter, which would allow the user to choose the outside area from which the air is drawn. The outside conditions may be that dense smoke is on one side of your building while the air is clear at the other side. Having the ability to choose from where your air is drawn could make a big difference in your survival.

FRESH AIR VALVE POSITION DETAIL

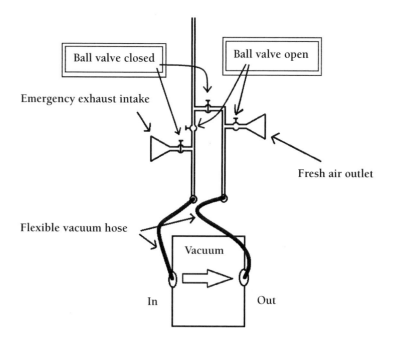

EMERGENCY EXHAUST VALVE POSITION DETAIL

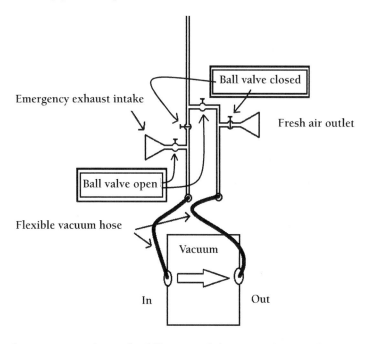

Outside air source
pipe from top side

Ball valve closed

Emergency exhaust intake

Fresh air outlet

Ball valve open

Flexible vacuum hose

Vacuum

In

Out

The emergency exhaust should be run only long enough to expel any gases, and then the valves should be quickly returned to the fresh air positions.

Parts List for the Drum Vac Air Pump

1. One piece of 3/4-inch plywood, 24 x 36 inches (or larger)
2. One drum-style wet/dry vacuum cleaner (with HEPA filter)
3. One 10-foot length of 1 1/4-inch PVC pipe
4. Three 90-degree "L" fittings
5. Four ball valves
6. Three T fittings
7. One roll of duct tape
8. One small can of PVC pipe glue
9. Five 1 1/2-inch PVC conduit straps (or similar)

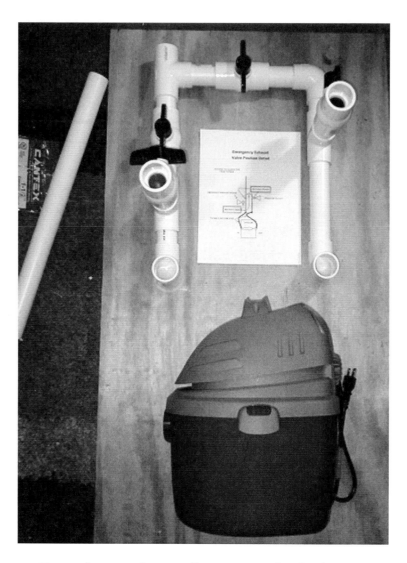

Even when purchasing all-new parts, this fresh air pump with HEPA filter should cost under $100 and can service any shelter with a positive airflow of 130 cubic feet per minute (7,800 cubic feet per hour), which can meet the needs of many people.

Here's how it all goes together:

- Following the HEPA filter installation instructions from Chapter 5, "Shelter-in-Place Emergency Air Management," seal the filter and tank of your vacuum cleaner.
- Lay out the piece of 3/4-inch plywood approximately 24 x 36 inches, to which you'll mount the air-intake manifold and vacuum.
- Using the diagrams from the previous pages, lay out your 1 1/4-inch PVC fittings.
- Measure and cut the length of 1 1/4-inch PVC pipe to join the fittings. The unit uses two 4 1/2-inch lengths of pipe for the two top horizontal runs, four 3 1/2-inch lengths of pipe for the vertical runs, two 3 1/2-inch lengths for the middle horizontal runs, and one 8 1/2-inch length for the right-side vertical run.

- Carefully glue and press all the fittings together.
- Use the five 1 1/2-inch conduit straps to secure the air manifold to the board above the vacuum unit.
- Place both ends of the vacuum hose that came with the vacuum into the in/out ports of the unit.
- Cut the hose where it centers between the manifold ends.
- Using duct tape, insert, secure, and seal the flexible hose ends into the open manifold ends.

- Carry the board to your shelter and affix it to a central wall to be permanently plumbed to your air-intake pipe.
- Copy and affix the "Emergency Valve Position" pages to your plywood board for everyone's reference in an emergency.

The greatest benefit to using this vacuum air pump system is in the availability of HEPA filters. It would be a good idea to have a large stock of replacement filters in case your buried bunker site happens to be in a nuclear fallout zone.

With this vacuum "air pump" system, the tank/filter should not be filling up with excessive dirt like a vacuum "cleaner" used in housecleaning. The filters will simply be catching dust in the air before it reaches the inside of your shelter. Virtually all models of drum vacuums should have the HEPA filter available, but you should investigate before purchasing a new vacuum for this purpose.

Using the calculation charts in Chapter 5, measure all

buried bunkers and figure the amount of available air. Knowing exactly how much time you and your group can safely remain inside your sealed bunker may become an important security concern. For example, if you suspect that the vacuum air pump might be heard from outside the bunker when turned on and know that you are able to go for two and a half hours without the air pump running, there just might be enough time for the group of thieving hooligans outside your door to pass by without noticing your position. Staying quiet, calm, and collected will help maintain your security and conserve limited air.

The vacuum cleaner air pump can and should be used when there are no threats to the shelter present, but when your immediate area is under scrutiny by an invading force or scouting patrol, the system should be shut down to ensure silence and safeguard your position. Take the time now to determine the interior dimension of your shelter in cubic feet and know your limitations.

For some preppers who scuba dive or have had family members on oxygen therapy, there may indeed be the opportunity to outfit the shelter with supplemental oxygen tanks. Make certain that everyone in the shelter is properly trained in both how to use and calculate airflow rates for the equipment you own. For the rest of us without scuba tanks, having a quieter, hand-operated air pump can make the difference between remaining concealed and being discovered. Then again, once your shelter has been discovered, turning on the electric pump may not matter since the sound of the motor is no longer an issue.

Under everyday circumstances when there is no threat present, it is generally considered safe to open the doors, vents, and hatches and freely move in, out, and about your underground shelter while either working your camp or stocking goods. Once you have moved into the shelter and closed the doors, however, it is vital to everyone's survival that at least one of your group be awake and alert at all times, day and night. It is risky for a solo prepper or a couple to disregard this protocol.

Even in a moderately sized shelter with what you may consider to be ample air, an alarm clock should be set to wake you at regular intervals so you can turn on the air pump. This is usually the plan most preppers have adopted for themselves anyway. Moving into the underground shelter would indicate the presence of a threat, and a watch duty has most likely already been established and put in place. If you don't have a 24-hour-watch schedule, you need to make one. In addition to being watchful for outside threats, the watchman must be certain fresh air is being pumped into the shelter during his watch so that the others can get a good night's rest without worry. While in a closed shelter, everyone's life depends on the watchman properly operating the air pump.

It may be of interest to note that multiple studies of over-the-road truckers have found that our bodies' sleep clocks to be on a 5-hour sleep schedule rather than the 8–10 hour schedule most people live by. This sleep schedule held true even under stressful, nonstop working conditions that most long-haul truckers experience while being confined to a small cabin area for long periods.

Living in your underground bunker will not be an easy road for most. It is likely that your shelter is smaller than you'd hoped for or that you have more people to protect than you'd originally counted on. Whatever your situation happens to be, keeping the air moving through the shelter with an air pump that exchanges the inside air with outside air will keep everyone drier, healthier, and alive.

High-humidity levels will make most people uncomfortable and can even trigger asthma attacks in some individuals. Expect the underground shelter to be cold, wet, and cramped, and make adjustments in how you live. The cold can be addressed with extra clothing, blankets, and bedding. Keep your sleeping bag rolled and stashed in your bug-out bag. Sleeping bags develop their own humidity issues, which will only worsen inside the bunker. Have extra sweaters or sweatshirts for everyone so they can wear layers. The aboveground shelter will not be much better.

Here again, having an electric heater should be considered a luxury item and only installed if your shelter is hardwired to the power grid via your house or other outbuilding. The safest heating source is electricity, since it will not consume precious air. All open-flame heaters should be saved for outside use and never used in a sealed shelter. Do not sacrifice the power used for the air-ventilation system in exchange for electric heat. Use electric heat only when you have more than enough power. As long as there are no outside threats to be concerned about, an outside or even an isolated and buried generator can provide electricity for an electric space heater that will not only heat your shelter but will also help in drying the air.

Perhaps the only negative aspect to this system is that the vacuum becomes a containment vessel of radioactive or other dangerous filtered particles, and it is positioned inside your shelter. This is still the lesser of two evils, since the alternative is allowing particles to be breathed in. Under extreme conditions, keep children as far away as possible from the vacuum unit.

9

BATHROOM FAN AIR PUMP

One of the easiest fans to convert for use in the home-built bunker is the bathroom exhaust fan, picked up at almost any home improvement store or, in the event of an emergency, salvaged from your bathroom. It is relatively inexpensive, uses very little electricity, and is not too loud, pushing approximately 50 cubic feet per minute. The negative aspect of using this type of fan as a shelter air pump is found in the unit's specifications. The motor is *not* engineered for continuous operation and cannot be expected to last or perform if subjected to continuous use for long periods. Anyone who's had to replace a bathroom fan would know just how long this actually is and would also be familiar with the noise the fan makes when it goes bad.

Do your math! Depending on the size of the shelter and the number of people inside, a bathroom fan may or may not be adequate for your continued use. Two or more of these units may be needed to keep up with your fresh air needs or at least offer an alternate air pump to keep any one fan from being run continuously.

Remember, since this is an electric fan, any disruption in your supply of electricity is a disruption in your supply of air. Act accordingly.

This type of fan was originally designed to be used as an exhaust fan and to have the intake port wide open. It needs to be adapted to connect to either a 3- or 4-inch PVC pipe. To make the necessary changes, you'll need a few more things from the home improvement store. The following is your complete shopping list for the bathroom fan air pump.

- Bathroom exhaust fan
- Two-way PVC pipe flange 3–4 inches
- One roll of metal duct tape (aluminum tape)
- Two pieces of 3/4-inch plywood approximately 14 x 14 inches
- A dozen or more wood screws 8 x 1 1/4 inches
- Tube of silicone caulk
- Sandpaper (80 grit)
- One grounded electric cord end (male)

The fan I used was a Broan Model 688, which came with an attractive grill we will not be using. The air-intake side of the fan's housing, where the grill would have been, measures about 7 1/2 inches square. Using one of the 14-inch square plywood boards, cut a 7 1/2-inch square hole out of the center. Fit the plywood over the fan and screw it into place through the holes provided in the inner edge of the plywood 7 1/2-inch square cut (below).

Using the metal tape, seal any holes or seams that would allow air to be sucked through by the fan, leaving only the fan-intake hole open (bottom photo). Be sure to also wrap the corner where the metal box meets the plywood (top photo). It is important to close off all areas that can provide air to the fan that is not vented to the outside air. You do not want the fan sucking in air from the shelter and simply recirculating it.

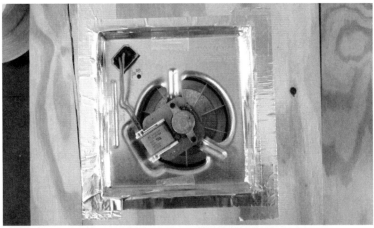

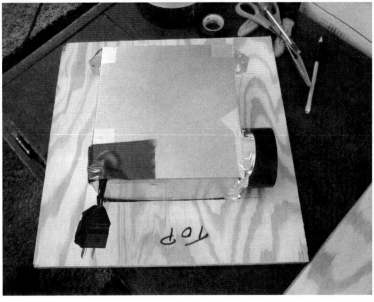

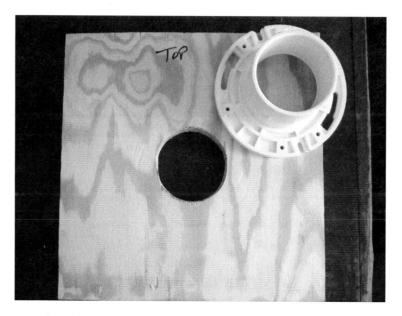

Place the second piece of 14 x14 plywood over the first and draw a 3 1/2-inch circle at the center. Cut out the 3 1/2-inch hole and sand all the edges.

Using the caulk to seal around the perimeter, place the second sheet of plywood with the 3 1/2-inch hole over the intake side of the first sheet of plywood with the fan set in it. Screw the two pieces of plywood together using four screws on each side.

Using the caulk again, run a bead around the flange of the PVC fitting. Place and screw down the fitting over the 3 1/2-inch hole.

The unit is now ready to fit over any 3- or 4-inch PVC intake pipe plumbed to your shelter. Once set in place, it may either be wired to a grounded circuit with a switch or wired to an extension cord. It should be noted that this fan may not have enough power to draw air through a dense in-line filter. Individuals wanting a filtered air system for their shelters will have to use the more powerful "vacuum cleaner" air pump system detailed in Chapter 8.

10

BLAST BUCKET
HAND-OPERATED
AIR PUMP

Regardless of the size of your sealed shelter, each person will be breathing approximately 400 cubic feet of air per day when at rest. When designing and building a hand-operated air pump, it is important to know how much air volume the pump will push. Comparing these two figures will allow you to know if the pump is large enough to keep up with the air needed in the shelter.

The smallest of the hand-operated air pumps detailed in this book is what I call the "Blast-Bucket." It moves approximately 1 cubic foot of air with each cycle. To move 400 cubic feet of air into your shelter with the Blast-Bucket, you'd have to cycle the pump 400 times (or 17 times per hour) over the course of a 24-hour day. *Remember, this must be done for each person in the shelter.* Two people in the shelter means 800 pump cycles per day (34 per hour), and three people in the shelter would require 1,200 cycles a day (or 51 cycles per hour). When there are more than two people in a small shelter, a larger pump might make better sense.

While there's no doubt that everyone will get some exercise (although limited) while in the shelter when operating any manual air pump, it's important to remember that the manual pump is simply a stopgap measure and cannot be continuously used for an extended period. It is virtually impossible to maintain an overpressure inside your bunker with a manually operated air pump. Additionally, all physical activity will use more oxygen and, therefore, diminish the overall end result of your physical efforts. Hopefully, your situation will improve enough so you can relocate if power is lost and you are reduced to using a hand-operated air pump to survive.

The Blast-Bucket is designed to be easy to build using manufactured parts readily found online or at big-box lumberyards, home centers, and surplus stores. You may already have some of the parts around the house ready for use. This air pump's small size makes it ideal for the one-to-three-man, small, buried shelter and is relatively quiet to operate.

It can be used as a primary air pump when there is natural ventilation occurring or as a secondary pump for either a shelter-in-place location or buried bunker. It may also be used with a HEPA filter located outside the shelter at the intake pipe.

The Blast-Bucket air pump is based on the simple design of a fireplace bellows and uses a standard 5-gallon pail. Similar to a fireplace bellows, this design has two check valves to ensure that air flows in the direction you want. This device is best used when set at a fixed location inside your bunker, being both attached and glued to the air-intake pipe and fastened to the floor using wood screws. Operating like a butter churn, it can be used while standing or seated.

As the PVC pipe handle is pulled up, the top valve closes and the bottom valve opens, allowing air to be pulled into the box chamber and the 5-gallon pail through the 3- or 4-inch intake pipe and filling the waterproof ALICE pack liner. Once the

Blast-Bucket hand-operated air pump.

pack is full, the handle is slowly pushed down, which will then close the bottom valve and open the top valve, allowing the air to flow into the room through the PVC pipe handle of the pump.

The design uses a soffit vent as the intake check valve, allowing for either the 3- or 4-inch PVC pipe to be used as the intake pipe. For this description I am using 3-inch schedule 40 PVC pipe for the air-intake pipe. Similar to the other designs in this book, a passive air exhaust pipe system is used.

PARTS LIST FOR THE BLAST BUCKET AIR PUMP

- 5-gallon pail (food grade, no lid)
- Soffit exhaust vent made by Lambro, item number L163W
- One 1 1/2-inch PVC check valve (flapper style)
- One 1 1/2-inch PVC pipe, 2-feet length
- One Oatey brand PVC 1 1/2- or 2-inch bell trap drain with 6 x 6 top
- One surplus military ALICE pack waterproof liner
- One sheet of 3/4-inch 4 x 8 plywood
- PVC glue
- Four machine bolts with wing nuts and washers, 1/4 x 1 1/2 inches
- Two large stainless steel hose clamps (6 inch and 7 inch)
- One 1 x 8-inch pine board, 8 feet long
- 8d finish nails
- Tube silicone caulk
- One 3- to 4-inch pipe flange

Note: Depending on your situation, building two or more air pumps is smart; having backups will keep you breathing if the first pump wears out or fails. Keeping several waterproof liners as replacements will also be a big plus when the first wears out.

BUILDING THE BLAST BUCKET AIR PUMP

1. Using a jigsaw, cut a round hole in the bottom of the 5-gallon pail to insert the Lambro soffit exhaust vent. Remove the 4-

inch adapter to the vent and discard. Set the vent inside the pail with the finished vent facing up and the vent bottom in the hole at the bottom of the pail. The vent should be seated tight to the bottom of the pail (top photo). Use the setscrews included in the vent package to hold the vent in place and then turn the pail over, resting the top rim on the floor (bottom photo). Caulk around the seam between the pail's bottom and the outside of the vent—this needs to be an airtight seal. The soffit vent is the air pump's intake check valve.

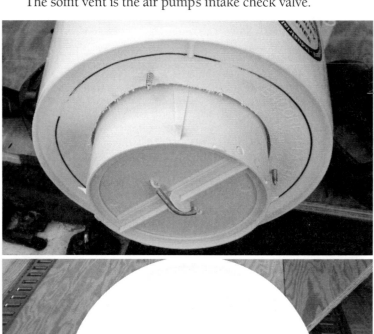

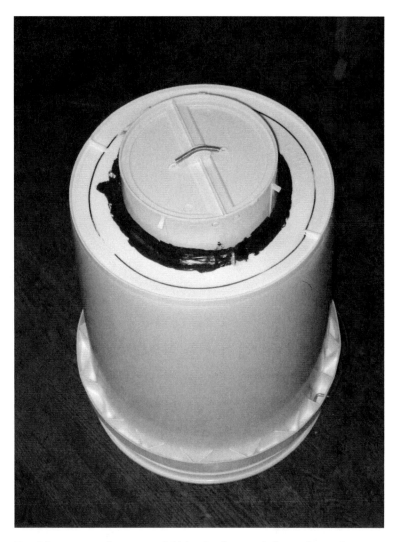

2. Measure and cut one 3/4-inch plywood disc, about 9 inches in diameter with a 1 1/2-inch hole at the center.
3. Find the center of the bottom of the waterproof bag and cut a 2-inch-diameter hole.
4. Line up and layer the center holes in the plywood disc, waterproof bag, and bell trap, and drill four 1/4-inch holes (one at each corner) to sandwich them together.

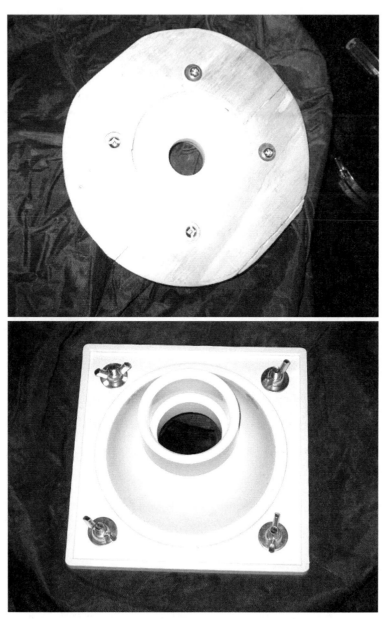

5. Build a 13-inch square box, 8 inches tall using the 1 x 8 board and the plywood.

6. Cut a round hole in the top of the wooden box large enough for the back of the soffit vent to pass through and allow the bottom of the 5-gallon pail to rest on the top of the box.

7. Cut a 3-inch round hole in one of the sides of the wooden box and screw the 3- or 4-inch PVC flange fitting in place over the hole.

8. Set the 5-gallon pail in place and centered in the hole at the top of the box, and screw it down tight through the inside bottom of the pail (you will have to back out the soffit vent screws to allow the bottom of the pail to be flush with the top of the box). Be sure the pail is tight and secure to the top of the box.

9. Place the open end of the waterproof bag over the top of the 5-gallon pail and let the wooden disc rest at the bottom of the pail. Fold the excess end of the bag down and over the outside of the pail and slip the stainless steel hose clamp over the rim. Use the two stainless steel hose clamps to evenly clamp the bag around the perimeter of the pail's rim (see photo below). It may be necessary to evenly pleat the fabric as it is placed and clamped around the rim. *Note:* Four self-adhesive felt pads can be used on the face of the disc that might come in contact with the intake vent inside the 5-gallon pail. Roll the excess end of the waterproof bag up to the clamp or rim.

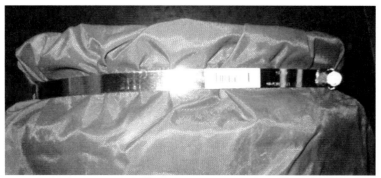

11

BRUTE BLASTER
HAND-OPERATED
AIR PUMP

Larger shelters with more people will need bigger fresh air pumps, especially when the primary electric pump cannot be used. Larger pumps simply move more air. While the Blast-Bucket air pump detailed earlier is useful as a secondary pump for small underground bunkers sheltering one to three people, it does not have the capacity to keep up with the air required for long periods.

The best up-sized buckets I have seen available are the Rubbermaid Brute series of round trash cans. They are, by far, the sturdiest and most durable available and come in various sizes for the prepper's needs. The next size up from the 5-gallon pail is the Brute 10-gallon can. By using a 10-gallon Brute can along with a 5-gallon pail, two soffit vents can eliminate the PVC pipe handle. Cut and place a soffit vent check valve in the bottom of both pails and bridge the rims with another waterproof ALICE pack liner or even a duffle bag with the bottom cut out. Finish by mounting the larger Brute can on a wooden box, similar to the Blas-Bucket, and placing a handle on the bottom of the 5-gallon pail. In the end you'll have an air pump pushing about 2 cubic feet per blast, which is about twice the volume of the Blast-Bucket.

The following chart shows my recommendation for what size secondary pump is needed depending on the size of your group. *Note:* These numbers are estimates based on the capacity of the buckets and the added capacity of the extended bellows. Full strokes will yield a little more, while half strokes can yield considerably less air movement.

Bucket Size (gallons)	Approximate Air Moved (per stroke)	Suggested Max. People
5	1 cubic foot	1–3
10	2 cubic feet	Up to 4
32	6.5 cubic feet	Up to 8
44	9 cubic feet	Up to 10
55	11 cubic feet	10 or more

One huge benefit of a larger group of people is in having the added strength and endurance to operate the hand air pumps in a lock-down situation without electricity. Having a shelter that's far bigger than needed is desirable as well.

It is important to note that there are few hand-operated air pumps that can keep up with continued air use in a sealed shelter. Oxygen levels must always be figured in to be safe. The use of any hand-operated air pump should be considered temporary at best, and it should only be used until all the occupants can be safely evacuated from the shelter.

The concept of the Blast-Bucket pump can be applied to any size bucket or drum. In an emergency, you can use any trash can or pail in a similar fashion. If you do not have the duffle bag or waterproof ALICE pack liner, you can use a heavy-duty trash bag. If you don't have the stainless steel clamps, you can use duct tape and wire. If you don't have the check valves, you can make one out of duct tape or even patches of leather cut from a jacket or handbag.

12

AIR FILTERS
AND GAS MASKS

As previously stated, HEPA filters are able to remove 99.97 percent of particles as small as .3 micron in size from the air (1 micron equals one-millionth of a meter). Someone with good eyesight can see a particle down to about 40 microns.

The HEPA filter can be used in your vacuum cleaner air pump as well as an in-line filter with the hand-operated pumps. For any prepper anticipating a nuclear, radiological, or biological attack in the region of his shelter, the HEPA filter is the long-term solution, with the only alternative being relocation.

Building your own air pump and learning how to safely manage the air in your shelter will keep you and your group breathing easy as long as the air outside the shelter is good. If the outdoor environment changes for the worse, you'll have to quickly adapt to survive. Some useful information may still be gleaned from mainstream media alerts. A report that an actual nuclear event has occurred in North America will be enough to spur you into immediate action. If you have been saving your supply of HEPA filters for "the big day," be sure you know where they are stowed so you can get them out immediately.

The key to knowing how to respond is knowing what the

outside threat is. HEPA air filters are the best and safest response to harmful particles in the air, including bacteria, viruses, dust, radioactive dust, anthrax, and other solids in the surrounding air.

The HEPA air filter will *not* filter out gases (neither poisonous nor nonpoisonous) and chemicals that are not solids in the form of particles in the air. For these items, the only safe response will be to use a gas mask with a chemical, biological, radiological, and nuclear (CBRN) filter.

The best course of action, when it has been determined that the shelter is your base, is to have the HEPA filter installed and used at all times. An inspection and cleaning schedule should be made to ensure that the HEPA filter is kept clean and has no breaches or holes that would allow the infiltration of contaminated air into the living area of the shelter. This schedule would vary depending on the region and location of the shelter. Locations in the desert southwest, where it is dry and dust storms are common, might require weekly inspections, while moist and humid areas, where dust is uncommon, might suffice with monthly inspections.

Most HEPA filters can be cleaned and reused several times, but hard cleaning can diminish their ability to maintain the HEPA filtration standard. Extra care must be taken to not puncture the paper-like filter membrane, and only soft cloth should come in contact with the filter. Knowing that your HEPA filter is clean, in good condition, and already installed in your vacuum cleaner air pump means that, in the event a nuclear detonation occurs, you can concentrate on other issues before seeking shelter from the fallout in your bunker. HEPA filters are expensive, as well, sometimes costing as much as the vacuum they fit. However, despite the cost, having several backup filters is always a good idea.

The following chart details the size of some common particles and threats measured in microns showing what the HEPA filter is able to protect you against. Note that the chart indicates particles smaller than the HEPA can filter, some as small as 0.001 microns. The HEPA can only filter particles down to 0.3 micron in size. This accounts for the HEPA not reaching 100-percent efficiency.

Particle Type	Particle Size (in microns)
Eye of a needle	1,240
Beach sand	100–10,000
Pollens	10–1,000
Fiberglass insulation	1–1,000
Grain dust	5–1,000
Dust mites	100–300
Sawdust	30–600
Tea dust	8–300
Ground coffee	5–400
Human hair	5–200
Cement dust	3–100
Red blood cells	5–10
Spores	10–30
Spider web	2–3
Insecticide dust	0.5–10
Anthrax	1–5
Yeast cells	1–50
Black carbon dust	0.2–10
Atmospheric dust	0.001–40
Copier toner	0.5–15
Bacteria	0.3–60
Wood smoke	0.2–3
Oil smoke	0.03–1
Tobacco smoke	0.01–4
Powdered sugar	0.0008–0.005
Pesticides/herbicides	0.001
Carbon dioxide	0.00065
Oxygen	0.0005
Viruses	.005–0.3

One excellent source for HEPA filters that cap 4-inch pipes is found online at International Growers Supply, Inc. The company carries a line of HEPA filters and in-line air pumps that are typically used in commercial organic greenhouses but can be adapted for use here. They also have larger diameter filters available for high-volume applications. By plumbing an air-intake pipe using 4-inch PVC along an outside wall and adding a 90-degree turn into your shelter, this 4-inch HEPA pipe filter can restrict the particle containment to the outdoors rather than allowing the particles to accumulate in your vacuum cleaner.

This can be done when planning your bunker or shelter-in-place location. By using the 4-inch HEPA pipe cap filter and another HEPA filter inside the vacuum unit, you'll effectively have a safer two-stage filtration system. In a similar fashion, this can be used as an outdoor filter for your Blast-Bucket or other hand-operated air pump.

Be certain to check the specifications and language used on any HEPA filter you purchase. Many are not actually HEPA filters but close imposters! Language like "HEPA-type filter" may indicate that the unit does not meet the 99.97 percent HEPA standard. All filters look alike and can easily be confused for the real thing. I have seen some filters advertised as HEPA style that are rated to only 90 percent efficiency. How would you like a glass of water that's only 90 percent filtered? HEPA filters are not inexpensive compared to other filters that at a glance may appear to be exactly the same. Purchase your HEPA filters from reputable companies. You might pay a bit more, but you'll get what you bargained for.

GAS MASKS

Among Leonardo da Vinci's numerous inventions is one not often talked about, what is believed to be the world's first gas

A 4-inch HEPA filter from International Grower Supplies is an excellent filter for your shelter.

mask. What may be even more surprising is that it has not changed much since he first suggested it in the 16th century. As a precautionary measure to guard against a powdered toxic weapon he had designed, da Vinci advised covering the nose and mouth with a fine cloth dipped in water. This method of protection can still be as effective today as it was then. In fact, it is still recommended as the best course of action when you don't have a mask or breathing apparatus.

The gas mask itself has gone through many changes in design as newer materials were developed that better covered and sealed the mouth, nose, and eyes from poisons and irritants. What was at first made from a water-sealed canvas fabric and glass is today made from a pliable butyl rubber and soft silicone with acrylic lenses. The newer military and commercial masks offer the wearer more comfort and a better seal against leaks. Unfortunately, the less-expensive civilian gas masks are far less durable and don't offer the same level of comfort or protection. As with any piece of equipment being considered for purchase, buying the best you can afford will pay off when you really need it, especially if you plan to exit your shelter during any of the poor-air events discussed above.

You must pay equal attention to your stock of gas mask filters. The best and latest gas mask filters are referred to as CBRN (chemical, biological, radiological, nuclear). You should also keep on hand special-use filter cartridges, available in a wide assortment of models. It is up to each individual or group to decide which filters should be kept in reserve at the shelter.

The chart at the top of the following page lists the type and color code used for the variety of gas mask cartridges available.

The biggest difference between the HEPA filter and the CBRN gas mask filter is that, while the HEPA filters only particles in the air, the CBRN can block particles, gases, and chemicals. This makes the CBRN the best all-around protection to have, but it comes at a high price. Many of the canisters for the CBRN masks cost well over $100 apiece and typically will only last about 45 minutes in an area of a high-active threat, while a HEPA filter can last much longer, in certain instances protecting you for months.

Contaminant	Color Coding on Cartridge/Canister
Acid gases	White
Hydrocyanic acid gas	White with 1/2 inch green stripe completely around the canister near the bottom.
Chlorine gas	White with 1/2 inch yellow stripe completely around the canister near the bottom.
Organic vapors	Black
Ammonia gas	Green
Acid gases and ammonia gas	Green with 1/2 inch white stripe completely around the canister near the bottom.
Carbon monoxide	Blue
Acid gases & organic vapors	Yellow
Hydrocyanic acid gas and chloropicrin vapor	Yellow with 1/2 inch blue stripe completely around the canister near the bottom.
Acid gases, organic vapors, and ammonia gases	Brown
Radioactive materials, except tritium & noble gases	Purple (magenta)
Pesticides	Organic vapor canister plus a particulate filter
Multi-Contaminant and CBRN agent	Olive
Any particulates - P100	Purple
Any particulates - P95, P99, R95, R99, R100	Orange
Any particulates free of oil - N95, N99, or N100	Teal

The newer term *CBRN* replaces *NBC* (nuclear, biological, and chemical) and *ABC* (atomic, biological, and chemical). The "R" for "radiological" was added to differentiate between radioactive dirty-bomb particles and radioactive fallout particles from a nuclear fission or fusion bomb. The useful service life of these filters varies widely, based on the conditions at the scene. A heavy assault or concentration of chemical, biological, radiological, or nuclear particles in your immediate area could cause the service life of the filter to be very short. Here again, having a supply of gas mask cartridges available as backup is wise. Furthermore, having a gas mask for everyone will allow your group to vacate the shelter and bug out if you get caught in a threat hot spot.

All CBRN filters have a shelf life and can go bad. When exposed to air, the active chemicals can absorb humidity and become unable to absorb the airborne threats they were designed to filter. Keeping the filters sealed and in a cool, dry, and stable environment will keep them serviceable past their shelf life, but a filter that has been opened and sitting on a shelf will most likely be useless in an emergency.

One option for those who have CBRN canister filters available is to use them at your air-intake pipe instead of on your gas mask. This can be done by connecting the 40mm threaded filters to a 1 1/2-inch PVC intake pipe using two hose clamps and a 1 1/2-inch inside dimension rubber hose. By doing this, a single cartridge can be shared by everyone in the shelter. This may prove to be better when the threat is not highly concentrated. However, the filter's life expectancy will still be a variable.

Under some conditions another alternative to this would be to cover the air intake pipe at the surface with a small open-top box covered by a damp cloth. Your objective here is to keep the dust down as much as possible. It would also be desirable in high-threat areas to have everyone wear masks while sitting quietly inside the shelter until the threat dissipates.

All gas mask filters will eventually become saturated and lose their ability to filter. In fact, even when newly opened, the cartridge will not be 100-percent effective. It will simply reduce

Using a 1 1/2-inch flexible coupling, you can attach a CBRN gas mask filter to a 1 1/2-inch air-intake pipe.

the level of gases or chemicals that reach the user. So, the user will be able to smell and taste whatever the threat is to some extent. The first clue that the cartridge is reaching saturation will be an increase in the discomfort and the effects the agent is having on the wearer. Again, the greater the concentration in your area, the shorter the life expectancy of your gas mask filter.

If you do choose to venture outside during the height of a nuclear fallout event or gas or chemical attack, wear the CBRN mask and be completely covered with a rain poncho, rain suit, or plastic trash bag, and gloves. Get the task completed quickly. While still outside, keeping your mask in place, remove the exposed clothes outside your shelter's entrance, taking extra care to keep the outside of your protective garments away from you at all times. Discard or leave the used outerwear outside and step back into your shelter with your mask still on.

It will be gases and chemicals that create the biggest threat inside your sealed shelter. Identifying the correct threat will not be easy. It will be your nose and eyes that give you the first clues that your shelter is under attack by a gas or chemical. Develop your own emergency action plan (EAP) and train everyone in the proper response to strange chemical smells, burning or watering eyes, or visible smoke in the shelter. During a real attack, your survival will depend on how swiftly you identify the threat and take action.

All risks are measured by the amount of time you are directly exposed to the threat and the level

Proper protective equipment for outside the shelter includes gas mask, coveralls, footwear, and gloves.

Sample Emergency Action Plan (EAP)

If anyone inside the shelter notices smoke or haze, experiences burning eyes or uncontrollable watering eyes, or develops an uncontrollable runny nose for no apparent reason, follow this emergency action plan!

- Alert everyone that a chemical attack might be in progress.

- Shut down or reverse the air pump flow. (This will be when you wish you had plumbed for the flow reversal.)

- Everyone in the shelter immediately dons masks and gets their CBRN filters ready to be opened. (You may not want to open the sealed filter until the attack is confirmed, but a smoke-filled shelter would be good confirmation.)

- Have an armed observer look and listen for confirmation of attack and then confirm the shelter's security by checking that the doors are closed and locked.

- Run the reverse flow until the smoke clears.

- If smoke cannot be blown out, shut down the air pump and close off all intake and exhaust ports.

- Once the attack has been confirmed, if your shelter has been cleared of smoke, gas masks may not be immediately necessary, but anyone suffering from the effects should deploy the CBRN filter.

- Start your air-use countdown clock.

- Periodically test the air pump to see if the attack canisters/grenades have dissipated.

- Ready your armed egress and counterattack or escape through a well-hidden escape tunnel.

or concentration of the agent to which you were exposed. Children are at a higher risk level than adults. Keep your kids inside and protected.

The sample emergency action plan on the previous page should be modified to fit your personal situation and can be as long or short as you require. Your plan should be posted where everyone is forced to look at it from time to time.

If you are caught without gas masks, you could offer everyone in the shelter a cool, moist towel to cover their faces and to breathe through, which will help a bit. However, typically under these circumstances, there is little that can be done without additional equipment. Having a gas mask for everyone in your shelter will allow additional time to execute your response. Either way, you will be leaving the shelter if the attack is prolonged and if attackers decide that they are

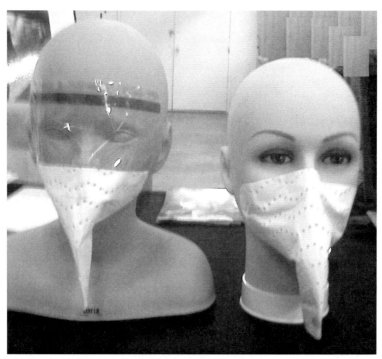

The Readi Mask is an affordable alternative to the gas mask.

coming in to get you. However, it will be a lot easier to greet them with gunfire if you're wearing your mask and not having to wipe your eyes.

A company called Global Safety First has recently developed an interesting alternative to expensive gas masks. Using a HEPA-like material, the Readi Mask offers a short-term, disposable mask that's effective against viruses, dust particles, bacteria, and most other airborne particulates that a HEPA filter would protect against. What's interesting is that the mask is simple to use and relatively inexpensive. An adhesive around the perimeter sticks directly to the wearer's face and to itself, creating a seal that prevents contaminated air from bypassing the filter. There are two versions of the mask, including one with an integrated eye protective shield. It is also available in child size. I see this as a cost-effective alternative to expensive particle masks, especially when the threat is of the type when sheltering in place is advisable.

13

SOME OTHER VARIATIONS

The few air pump designs outlined so far in this book are simple and inexpensive for anyone concerned about managing the airflow in their underground shelters. Seeing these designs and what can be done at home, many preppers may be able to modify other common items and design a better air pump than what I have detailed here. As long as preppers know the limits of their shelters and have a system to meet their needs, they're covered. There is certainly more than one way to do this, as there is no one-size-fits-all plan. In the end, the only thing that matters is the safety and survival of those being sheltered.

The preppers I have met over the years have been ingenious in coming up with clever ways of doing things. We have long had our off-grid power provided by solar panels and generators that both charge and offer 12V DC and 120V AC current, depending on what our needs happen to be. For us, solar power has been more efficient when charging 12V DC batteries and then using an AC inverter for our needs. Rarely have I ever directly connected to batteries for my DC needs. That being said, I have toured many off-grid homes wired for and powered with 12V DC. In fact, there is a large selection of 12V

DC appliances available for the trucking industry that many preppers use off-grid at home.

For the 12V DC preppers out there, I have seen many 12V DC high-output fans. One that got my attention was found on-line at Amazon for about $20. It was a 14-inch reversible, automotive radiator fan that could be readily adapted to use as an air-supplying fan in a buried shelter. The fan I looked at moved a huge amount of air at 2,000 cubic feet per minute. The handy 12V DC prepper could easily build a plywood box to house the fan and to which plumbing fittings could be attached. An even handier prepper might add a 14 x 14-inch HEPA home furnace filter to the box as well.

In my search for shelter air pumps, I came across some other very good ideas, including the use of a discarded leaf blower with a hand crank attached where the engine once was. This, too, could be modified and used as a buried-shelter air pump. Then, for the prepper/machinist/welder, there is always the bicycle/turbine, belt-driven fan (illustrated on the next page) that can be put into service.

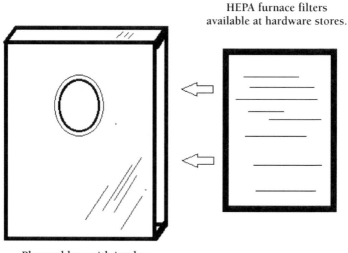

HEPA furnace filters available at hardware stores.

Plywood box with intake pipe PVC 3- to 4-inch ports.

Bicycle air pump

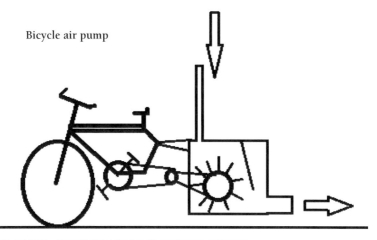

There are several HEPA vacuum cleaner filters that can be modified for use in a home shelter.

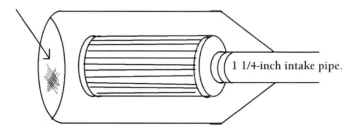

Screened cover.

1 1/4-inch intake pipe.

Air-intake pipe with Hoover HEPA cartridge
covered with 4-inch-diameter PVC.

As long as there is enough fresh air moving through your
shelter for the number of people inside, it's a good pump.
Make it better by adding a HEPA filter.

In my research on HEPA filters, I found one that offers
multiple uses. The HEPA filter made for the Hoover Twin
Chamber and 201 model vacuums costs about $35 at this writ-
ing. Its shape, size, and design make it a good choice to place
directly over a 1 1/4-inch PVC intake pipe. With a little work,
a cover can be made to protect it from weather, bugs, and critters, making it an almost universal HEPA filter for the shelter.
It can also be used to add HEPA benefits to the Blast-Bucket.

14

FINAL THOUGHTS AND CONCLUSIONS

The citizens of the United States are often a forgotten group when it comes to underground protection from nuclear and other threats. Our government will be seeing to it that designated politicians and bureaucrats are protected and have the necessary supplies and equipment to see them through a worst-case scenario. Meanwhile, other countries are building underground shelters at breakneck speeds for their citizens. What is clear is that our future is up to us. While our government promotes dependency, only the independent thinkers will survive.

As a fellow prepper and survivalist, I wanted to offer simple plans and ideas that would help others get through the difficult times that might come our way. Even if you do not have an underground shelter today, you most likely have a vacuum cleaner or a bathroom fan. With what you know now, you could build a quick shelter at the last minute with whatever materials you have or could scavenge, and you would have the means to both supply and filter air for you and your family. If you found yourself without electricity, you'd certainly be able to find a 5-gallon pail or a trash can and devise an air pump. Even shelter-in-place preppers will be able to fashion an adequate air pump that filters radioactive or anthrax particles from the air.

I would urge everyone not to wait until then but rather to start now. Gather the items needed to build these air pumps or design your own. Be prepared to shelter in place or find a discreet location and build a shelter equipped with an air pump to protect you and your children from a worst-case scenario coming soon to a town near you.

Prepare now and breathe a sigh of relief.

AUTHOR'S NOTE

As if conventional warfare wasn't bad enough for preppers to consider, there are far more worrisome threats to be concerned about. These additional threats include nuclear bombs, chemical warfare, and biological and pandemic threats that can be either naturally occurring or engineered by man. You have few effective options to treat members of your group without a doctor and extensive medical supplies available. Sadly, people will die. At best, we can work to ease their discomfort and suffering as best we can. Prevention is still the best medicine we can practice. However, being ready for these types of extreme threats can be extremely expensive.

Some people will be able to put together chemical suits for their group, or at least a complete cover of some type, along with gas masks, in order to venture outside when necessary in a nuclear fallout event. For most of us, there will be little or no protection from nerve, blister, choking, or blood agents used against us. Fortunately, these types of attacks are generally intentionally directed at larger targets, and most preppers will not be considered a large enough threat for these weapons to be used against them. Being well hidden and remaining undiscovered will be the best deterrent against exposure.

Of all these threats, the U.S. military expects that the most likely to be used against its troops is a chemical attack, and that's what they have prepared for. This has helped the prepper greatly by making surplus chemical suits and masks available to civilians. For preppers who expect any of the threats listed above and also fear that their locations could be discovered, obtaining a chemical suit for each member of your group should be a priority. If such an attack occurs, anyone without a suit will have to be sheltered or removed from the affected area. For preppers with a chemical suit, actively defending your position to prevent or stop a chemical attack may save the others in your group.

Though all of these attacks are bad, nuclear fallout is the easiest to defend against in the short term with a sealed shelter and a HEPA filter, but the long-term effects on the environment would most likely force you from the area at some point. Likewise, any attack using airborne solids—such as anthrax, bacteria, or certain viruses—can be defended against using a HEPA filter. These types of threat will dissipate into the environment fairly quickly and do not require long-term protection. The rest of the threats, either gas or chemical in nature, will require a CBRN gas mask and suit for short-term protection.

This book addresses the quality management of the air inside your shelter. Like so many other concerns, there are related issues not detailed here that will require further study by the prepper. The proper use of chemical suits and the medical treatment for deadly agent exposures are just two of them. Prepare for the level of threat you expect!

When calculating the amount of usable air in a sealed room, I based my findings on a calculation of 21 percent of the total volume of air in the 400-cubic-foot room equaling the total amount of oxygen in the room. Then figuring the ratio of time and percentage of oxygen in the air, I determined when the 19.5 percent level of oxygen was reached with a 5 percent loss of oxygen with each breath.

Another way to determine the breathable air supply is to calculate the increase in carbon dioxide using this formula solving for time (T).

$$\frac{\text{(Total cubic feet of air in room)} \times (0.03)}{T = \text{(Number of people)} \times \text{(hourly production of } CO_2 \text{ per person)}}$$

All said, the end result is the same—your time is much shorter than most people would believe. The air of everyone who shelters in a sealed or confined area must be managed.

Depending on your situation, staying inside a buried shelter that has electric power may be the best overall option, and replacing the HEPA filter might become a necessity in heavy fallout areas. Ideally, the vacuum is a containment unit, but when the filter needs to be replaced and you don't have a spare vacuum and filter, there are few options left. Under these circumstances, have everything you'll need ready. Cover yourself with a poncho or chemical suit, and wear a HEPA particle mask or CBRN mask and gloves. Take the unit outside the shelter and far enough downwind from your intake and exhaust pipes for contamination not to be an issue. Do the replacement as quickly as possible and be certain to follow all the directions previously detailed.

Further study relating to these concerns is available through the FEMA Technological Hazards publications.

APPENDIX
Four Examples of U.S. Department of Defense Shelter Designs

   In 1961, the U.S. Department of Defense released the plans for seven nuclear fallout shelters to the general public. All seven plans were straightforward and offered hope to the "informed man" of 1961. Fortunately for us all, neither the shelters nor the common man were put to the ultimate test.

   Looking back at these plans today, what becomes painfully clear is that 1961's informed man did not fully understand the true level of threat that nuclear fallout represented. Most of the shelter plans depicted the average middle-class family wearing their Sunday-best clothing and hunkering down inside what may as well have been a family coffin. It's not really clear what the game plan was back then, but it appears that the shelters were just feel-good measures for the ill-advised. Most of the shelters were simply too small for more than one person to begin with and lacked commonsense planning as well. Cramming three people into a buried 4 x 4 x 8-foot wooden box for the duration of a nuclear fallout event without any adequate storage space for food and water is just poor planning. Aside from the lack of a HEPA filter on the air pump, any number of other issues would have driven the entire family out of the shelter and into the contaminated area, rendering the shelter virtually useless.

Of the plans released back then, four models remain redeemable in today's world. They are included here as potential shelter plans for one person or perhaps as an in-house shelter for children. By increasing their sizes, they would allow for more people to be sheltered. I have also made a few notes as to how I would improve and update these shelter plans.

Basement Concrete Block Shelter

GENERAL INFORMATION

This concrete block basement compact shelter will provide low-cost protection from the effects of radioactive fallout. It is intended to be installed belowgrade in a basement. Its principal advantages are simple design, speed of construction, ready availability of low-cost materials, and adequate protection against fallout radiation. By increasing the ceiling height to 6 feet or more, it could also serve as a dual-purpose room.

TECHNICAL SUMMARY

Space and Occupancy.—This shelter has about 52 square feet of area and 260 cubic feet of space and will provide shelter for four persons.

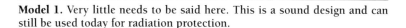

Model 1. Very little needs to be said here. This is a sound design and can still be used today for radiation protection.

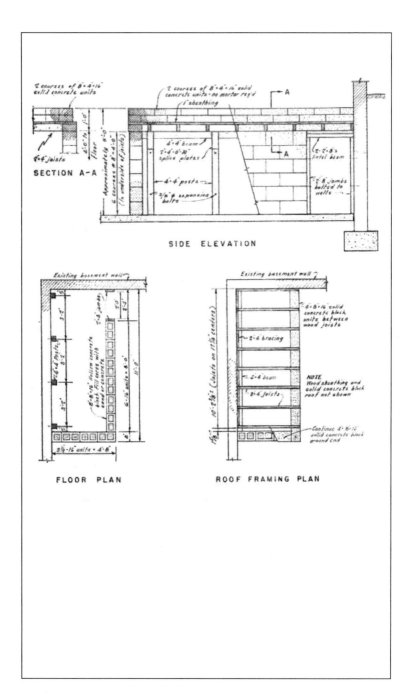

2 courses of 8·4·16 solid concrete units

2 courses of 8·4·16 solid concrete units - no mortar req'd
1" sheathing

4·4 beam
2·4·6·16 splice plates

2·2·8's lintel beam

SECTION A-A

4·4 posts

2·8 jambs bolted to walls

3/8" ∅ expansion bolts

SIDE ELEVATION

Existing basement wall

2·4 posts 3·5

2·6 jambs

8·8·16 hollow concrete block filled with sand or concrete

6·16 units 8·0

3½·16 units · 4·8'

FLOOR PLAN

Existing basement wall

4·8·16 solid concrete block units between wood joists

2·4 bracing

2·4 beam

2·4 joists

NOTE
Wood sheathing and solid concrete block roof not shown

10·2⅝'s (Joists on 11⅜ centers)

Continue 4·8·16 solid concrete block around end

ROOF FRAMING PLAN

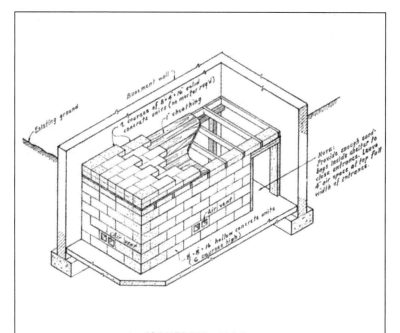

ISOMETRIC VIEW

Availability and Cost of Materials.—Most of the materials required to build this shelter are obtainable at local concrete-block plants and lumber yards. The cost of the materials for the basic shelter is estimated at $75 per shelter.

Fallout Protection Factor.—In most residences, the shelter will provide a protection factor of at least 100.

Blast Protection.—Although this shelter was designed primarily to provide fallout protection,

it would also provide some protection from flying debris associated with blast.

Ventilation.—Natural ventilation is provided by the airspace left at the entranceway after emergency closure, and the air vents in the shelter wall.

Construction Time.—Estimated construction time for the basic shelter is less than 20 man-hours.

Structural Life Expectancy.—The life expectancy of the shelter would be about the same as most types of residences.

CONSTRUCTION SEQUENCE

1. Lay out guidelines with chalk on basement floor for shelter walls. (See floor plan.)
2. Lay first course of block in a full bed of mortar. Vary thickness of mortar bed if basement floor is not level.
3. Continue to lay wall blocks. Corner of wall should be built up first, about three or four courses high, before laying blocks in remainder of wall. All blocks should be laid in a full bed of mortar. Where 8-inch blocks are required, cut 16-inch units in half with a hammer and chisel.
4. Fill cores of blocks with sand (or concrete) after three courses have been laid up.
5. Continue procedures indicated above in steps 3 and 4 until walls have been laid up to a height of 4 feet (six courses), and all cores have been filled with sand (or concrete).
6. Brush-coat all surfaces of lumber with water-repellent solution. Double brush-coat all edges. (Optional procedures. Desirable for wood preservation.)

7. Fasten wood posts and doorjambs to existing basement walls and shelter walls with expansion bolts. Use two bolts per post. (See side elevation.)
8. Place wall beam and door lintel beam in position and secure to posts with nails.
9. Place wood joists and bracing in position and secure together with nails. (See roof framing plan.)
10. Place portion of wood sheathing on top of joists. Nail wood sheathing to joists. (See isometric view.)
11. Place solid concrete masonry units on top of wood sheathing. No mortar is required between these units.
12. Continue procedures indicated above in steps 10 and 11 until roof covering has been completed.
13. Bags of sand or additional solid concrete blocks should be stored near entrance for emergency closure, but airspace of at least 4 inches should be left at top of closure for ventilation and air circulation.

BILL OF MATERIALS

(Ceiling height 4 feet)

Item	Quantity
8" x 8" x 16" hollow concrete masonry units*	65.
8" x 4" x 16" solid concrete masonry units*	135.
Mortar (prepared dry mix)	5 cubic feet.
Sand or concrete (for filling cores)	1 ton.
Sandbags	30.
4" x 4" x 3'8" wood posts (structural grade)	4.
2" x 8" x 3'8" wood posts (structural grade)	2.
2" x 8" x 2'4" wood beam (structural grade)	2.
4" x 4" x 10'3" wood beam (structural grade)	1.
1" wood sheathing	52 board feet.
2" x 4" x 4'8" wood joists (structural grade)	8.
4" x 4" x 10'3" wood beam (structural grade)	8.
2" x 4" wood bracing (structural grade)	10 linear feet.
¾" x 7" expansion bolts	12.
Sixteenpenny nails	2 pounds.
Sixpenny nails	2 pounds.
Water repellent (5 percent pentachlorophenol or equal), toxic to wood-destroying fungi and insects.**	1 quart.

*Units should be made with concrete having a density not less than 130 pounds/cubic feet.
**Optional.

Outside Semimounded Plywood Box Shelter

GENERAL INFORMATION

This shelter is designed to provide low-cost protection from the effects of radioactive fallout. Its principal advantages are ready availability of low-cost materials, ease and speed of construction, adequate protection from fallout radiation, and limited blast resistance.

TECHNICAL SUMMARY

Space and Occupancy.—The shelter in this design has 32 square feet of area and 128 cubic feet of space and will house three persons. See *"NOTE"*

after "Construction Sequence" for description of a size to house more persons.

Availability and Cost of Materials.—Most of the materials needed to build this shelter are obtainable at lumberyards. The nationwide average for cost of materials is about $75 per shelter, not including ventilation equipment.

Fallout Protection Factor.—A protection factor of about 500 is obtained if the earth cover is 2 feet deep, and a 2-foot thick entranceway shield is formed with bags of sand.

Blast Protection.—The shelter should be able to withstand a limited blast overpressure of 5 pounds per square inch.

Model 2. As shown, this wood-framed shelter is too small and light duty, but it can be modified for use today. Assigning one shelter per person and upgrading the timber to 4 x 4s or larger, placed 12 inches O.C., and sheathed with 3/4-inch plywood, a row of these can be built for several people. A single air pump can be centrally located and used for all. Each shelter could house one person along with his own food, water, and gear. Adjoining walls can be left open and a single entry used as access for all.

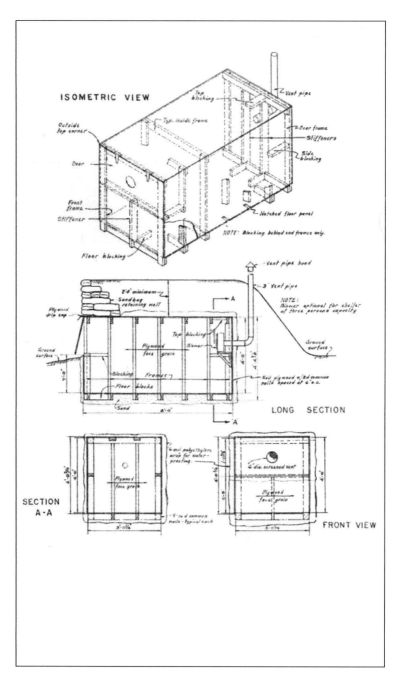

ISOMETRIC VIEW

LONG SECTION

SECTION A-A

FRONT VIEW

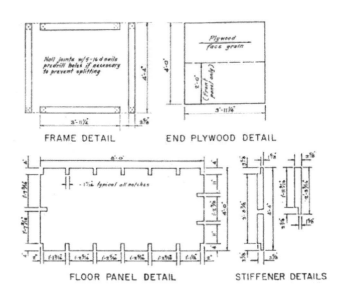

FRAME DETAIL   END PLYWOOD DETAIL

FLOOR PANEL DETAIL   STIFFENER DETAILS

Ventilation.—A 3-inch vent at the rear of the structure provides an essential opening to which a pipe extension can be attached. Hand-operated ventilation equipment should be used for more than three persons. The additional cost may be from $30 to $50. Air is exhausted through the airspace left in the entranceway closure.

Construction Time.—Tests have shown that one man working with simple excavating and construction tools can perform all necessary work in 20 man-hours. This time will be lessened by about 5 hours if lumberyards provide prefabricated plywood panels and sections.

Structural Life Expectancy.—The range is from 5 to 10 years depending on the humidity in the area, drainage characteristics of the terrain, and the effectiveness of the wood treatment (dip preferred) and the plastic wrapping.

CONSTRUCTION SEQUENCE

1. Cut plywood and lumber to size and notch before treating.
2. Dip lumber for 2 minutes or more in water repellent. A trough can be fashioned from a piece of polyethylene film and scrap lumber. Dip plywood in water repellent or give thorough brush treatment. Double brush-coat all cut edges.
3. Assemble the seven frames. (See longitudinal section drawing.)
4. Select a well-drained site. Excavate hole deep enough so that shelter floor will be at least 2 feet below ground surface and wide enough to permit nailing of plywood sides to frames from outside. Slope bottom of the trench so that shelter will be 2 inches higher at entrance than at rear. Lay a 2-inch sandbed for polyethylene moisture barrier.

5. Place polyethylene moisture barrier in excavation and cover bottom with a 4-inch layer of sand to prevent frames from breaking barrier. (Sec. A–A, Front View.)
6. Cut three floor blocks to size and tack to underside of floor panel. Place the seven frames approximately in place, imbedded so that the sand will be flush with the underside of the floor panel. Then pass the floor panel inside the frames and nail in place.
7. Toe the end and side panels on the edges of floor panel and nail securely; then nail the side and top blocking, and finally, nail the top panel overlapping both the side and end panels.
8. Pad the outside top corners of the shelter to prevent damage to the polyethylene moisture barrier. Wrap the shelter with the polyethylene.
9. Backfill with 2 feet of earth cover after forming a sandbag retaining wall over the entrance (see longitudinal section) and alongside entranceway.
10. Provide enough filled sandbags or solid concrete blocks for a closure 2 feet thick in the entrance.

11. As an alternative to digging a large hole as described in step 4 above, a somewhat smaller hole can be used if the shelter is assembled above ground and lowered gently into the hole. The shelter weighs approximately 400 pounds complete, or 260 pounds without ends and top. Care must be taken to avoid puncturing the polyethylene moisture barrier.
12. If blower is installed, it should be supported by blocking, or by a frame attached to the end panel with 2″ x 4″ stiffeners.

NOTE: The size of the shelter may be increased in width and height. There is no arbitrary limit to length but the plywood sheets must butt each other at a frame. To increase the width from 4′ to 6′ use 2″ x 6″ ceiling joists. To increase the width from 6′ to 8′ use 2″ x 8″ ceiling joists. To increase the height from 4′ to 6′ use 2″ x 6″ wall studs and floor joists. When increasing height or width the ceiling joists should rest directly on the wall studs and be secured to them by means of nailed ⅜-inch plywood gussets. Ceiling joists require a gusset on one side only. Floor joists require a gusset on each side. Use 12 sixpenny nails in each gusset. Six nails should be used in each of the joined pieces.

BILL OF MATERIALS
(For 4′ x 8′ size)

Item	Quantity
¾″ exterior plywood (Federal specification CS 45–60) or ½″ exterior plywood (Federal specification CS 122–60, group 1 or 2).	5 sheets.
2″ x 4″ x 10′ construction grade Douglas fir or equal	8 pieces.
2″ x 4″ x 8′ construction grade Douglas fir or equal	8 pieces.
4″ x 4′ plywood lumber (drip cap)	1 piece.
9 mil polyethylene film (16′ width)	20 feet.
Water repellent (5 percent pentachlorophenol or equal), toxic to wood-destroying fungi and insects.	2 gallons.
Eightpenny galvanized common nails	4 pounds.
Sixteenpenny galvanized common nails	3 pounds.
3″ diameter galvanized vent pipe	3½ feet.
Vent pipe cap	1.
3″ diameter 90° elbows	2.
Galvanized hinges	1 pair.
Flyscreen 7″ x 7″	1.
Sandbags	58.
Dry sand	3 tons.
Blower (optional, to be used with vent pipe, for 3-person size).	1.
Soil or sand (for shelter cover)	5 cubic yards.

FAMILY SHELTER SERIES   PSD F–61–5

Belowground Corrugated Steel Culvert Shelter

GENERAL INFORMATION

This shelter is designed to provide low-cost protection from the effects of radioactive fallout. Its principal advantages are that most of the structure is generally available as a prefabricated unit ready for lowering into an excavation and that it requires only simple connections and covering to complete the installation.

TECHNICAL SUMMARY

Space and Occupancy.—This shelter has 32 square feet of area and about 120 cubic feet of space (including the entranceway). It could provide space for three persons. The addition of a 4-foot length would provide for one more person.

Availability and Cost of Materials.—This type of shelter is available from steel culvert fabricators or their sales outlets in most population centers. This prefabricated shelter, including ventilation system, plastic wrap, and sandbags is designed to be sold for $150 or less, excluding delivery and installation.

Fallout Protection Factor.—When the entranceway is properly shielded as shown in the drawings, the protection factor should be greater than 500.

Blast Protection.—This shelter could be expected to withstand a limited blast overpressure of 5 pounds per square inch.

Ventilation.—A sheet metal intake vent 3 inches in diameter is provided together with a manual airblower for more than three persons. Air is vented through the sandbag closure at the entrance.

Installation Time.—One man working with hand excavation tools should be able to complete the excavation in less than 2 man-days. Two men will be needed to roll the shelter structure into the excavation from the point at which the shelter has been delivered. If lifting rather than rolling is necessary to transport the structure, four men will be required. Time for this phase will vary upward from 1 hour depending on distance of the move. It will then take one man 4 working days to complete the covering and installation phases.

Model 3. The kit for this round culvert pipe shelter design is no longer available, nor is the pipe it used. However, the idea is sound, and it can give preppers ideas about what can be done with large pipes and water tanks. When using a plastic water tank for this purpose, bulkheads should be used to strengthen the sidewalls at the midpoints of the walls. Remember that this design was intended to hold in the weight of the water, *not* to hold out the weight of the dirt.

Structural Life Expectancy.—The estimated life of this galvanized steel shelter will be at least 10 years under most soil conditions. Under normal conditions highway culverts of similar material have been known to last indefinitely with little maintenance.

CONSTRUCTION SEQUENCE*

1. Select well-drained site. The total area required, including the mounding, will be approximately 15' x 20'.
2. Use stakes to mark the corners of the area, and excavate. The hole required for the main shell is 5' x 9' x 2' deep, and the entrance requires an additional 2½' x 4' x 6''.
3. Line hole with plastic film wrap.
4. Lower galvanized steel shelter into place on supporting wood strips.
5. Assemble and install the vent pipe.
6. Cover shelter with plastic wrap.
7. Backfill and mound. Be sure the shelter is covered by at least 2 feet of packed earth. Depth may be checked with a wire probe. The mound should be covered with grass as soon as possible by sodding or seeding to prevent the protective soil from being eroded.
8. Place small sandbags inside the shelter. These are used to fill the entrance completely after the shelter is occupied.
9. 1-inch boards may be used on 2'' x 4'' blocks to provide a floor.

*This is a generalized construction sequence for a prefabricated steel culvert shelter. Detailed instructions are provided with the construction kit.

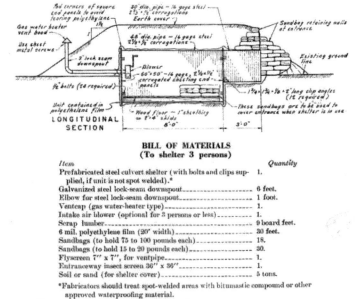

LONGITUDINAL SECTION

BILL OF MATERIALS
(To shelter 3 persons)

Item	Quantity
Prefabricated steel culvert shelter (with bolts and clips supplied, if unit is not spot welded).*	1.
Galvanized steel lock-seam downspout	6 feet.
Elbow for steel lock-seam downspout	1 foot.
Ventcap (gas water-heater type)	1.
Intake air blower (optional for 3 persons or less)	1.
Scrap lumber	9 board feet.
6 mil. polyethylene film (20' width)	30 feet.
Sandbags (to hold 75 to 100 pounds each)	18.
Sandbags (to hold 15 to 20 pounds each)	30.
Flyscreen 7'' x 7'', for ventpipe	1.
Entranceway insect screen 36'' x 36''	1.
Soil or sand (for shelter cover)	5 tons.

*Fabricators should treat spot-welded areas with bitumastic compound or other approved waterproofing material.

Aboveground Earth-Covered Lumber A-Frame Shelter

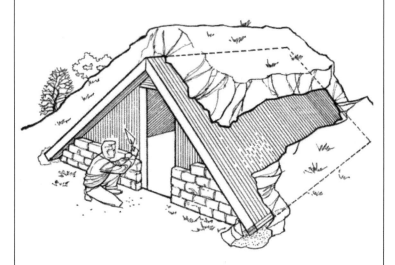

GENERAL INFORMATION

The purpose of this shelter is to provide protection for 10 persons from the effects of radioactive fallout at a location near but separate from a residence or other nearby buildings. The principal advantage of this shelter is that it can be erected without excavation in locations where there is poor drainage or where the ground water table is close to the surface. However, this shelter is not a low-cost structure. Footings or thrust ties are needed where the earth is soft or of poor bearing capacity.

TECHNICAL SUMMARY

Space and Occupancy.—This shelter provides almost 150 square feet of area and approximately 640 cubic feet of space. Although only a small portion of this area provides sufficient headroom for standing erect, practically the entire area can serve as sitdown space for 10 persons and storage space for supplies.

Model 4. Of the four plans shown here, this is my favorite. Even though it is shown as an aboveground shelter, the roof design can be used over a deep-cut trench and buried under 3 feet of earth when constructed with 2 x 8 or larger lumber. The gable ends can be used as access ports to tunnels or entries. This is a strong structure and could be used today.

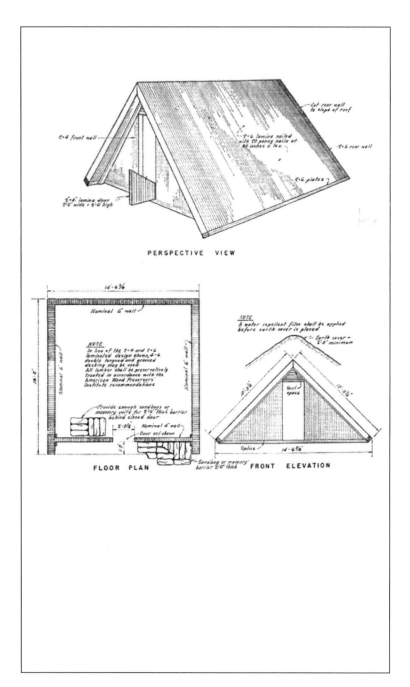

PERSPECTIVE VIEW

FLOOR PLAN

FRONT ELEVATION

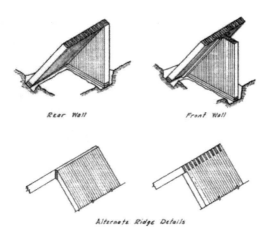

Rear Wall

Front Wall

Alternate Ridge Details

CONSTRUCTION DETAILS

Availability and Cost of Materials.—The pressure-treated lumber which is required is generally available at retail lumberyards. In certain areas it may be necessary to allow time for the treated lumber to be ordered and transported from stock at other locations. The estimated cost of materials is $550.

Fallout Protection Factor.—The recommended minimum earth cover of 2 feet with an entranceway and door shielded by a 2-foot thickness of sandbags, and the rear wall mounded will provide a protection factor of about 500.

Blast Protection.—While the basic function of this shelter is fallout protection, limited blast resistance of about 5 pounds per square inch of overpressure would be afforded by the heavy wood structure. The blast resistance would vary somewhat with the workmanship and materials but the laminated design tends to offset variations.

Ventilation.—Ducts for mechanical ventilation may be located in the ventspace over the doorway without involving structural change. Hand-operated ventilation equipment should be used.

Construction Time.—After materials are delivered at the jobsite, 4 man-days should be allowed for erecting the structure. Earth covering would require 4 additional man-days, without the use of power equipment.

Structural Life Expectancy.—The life expectancy of this shelter should be from 15 to 20 years.

CONSTRUCTION SEQUENCE

1. Assemble the materials at the shelter site.
2. Trench to subsoil for the wallplates as shown on the floor plan and details. Assemble plates in the trenches. (See construction details, rear-front walls.)
3. Begin at either end and erect roof wall members in pairs. (See alternate ridge details.) Progress to the opposite end, spiking laminations together. If 2″ x 6″ lamina are used, they should be nailed with twentypenny nails at approximately 30-inch spacing. If 4″ x 6″ decking lamina are used, they should be fastened together with 5/16-inch diameter spikes at approximately 30-inch spacing.
4. Erect the end walls as shown on the drawings with ends of the lamina cut flush with the roof wall top surface. The lamina should be spiked together in the same manner as the roof members.
5. The supporting structure is now complete. It should be covered with the polyethylene film and covered with earth. The earth cover should be started at the base of the roof walls and applied evenly to both sides. Next mound earth against the rear wall. The sandbags or masonry blocks are applied on both sides of the front wall to a thickness of 2 feet. A supply of filled sandbags or blocks should be stored inside the shelter to add to the protection afforded by the door.
6. Vegetation, riprap, or other means of holding the soil in place should be provided.
7. A duct for air intake will be required with the installation of the hand-operated blower. The intake duct may be located in the rear wall of the shelter and the air can be exhausted through the louvered ventspace over the doorway.
8. The door may be of heat- or blast-resistant construction, as manufactured commercially, or may be contrived by nailing 2″ x 4″ studs together to make a 4-inch-thick door. This then can be mounted with ordinary hinges and should be painted white.

BILL OF MATERIALS

Item	Quantity
Roof walls 2″ x 6″ x 10′	250 pieces.
Rear wall 2″ x 6″ x 8′	50 pieces.
Front wall 2″ x 4″ x 8′	40 pieces.
Plates:	
2″ x 6″ x 10′	10 pieces.
2″ x 4″ x 10′	3 pieces.
Fastenings:	
Fortypenny nails	10 pounds.
Twentypenny nails	30 pounds.
Water repellent—building felt or plastic film	150 square feet.
Bagged earth or masonry blocks for front wall shielding.	600 filled sandbags (30 pounds) or 176 concrete blocks (8″ x 12″ x 16″).
Blower, manually operated (rated at 30 cubic feet per minute).	1.
Intake pipe, galvanized (to be mounted through rear wall).	6 feet.
Flyscreen 7″ x 7″ (for intake pipe)	1.
Flyscreen 24″ x 24″ (to cover ventspace over door).	1.